The Institute of Chartered Accountants in England and Wales

BUSINESS AND FINANCE

For exams in 2014

Question Bank

ICAEW

www.icaew.com

Business and Finance
The Institute of Chartered Accountants in England and Wales

ISBN: 9780-8576-0684-6
Previous ISBN: 9780-8576-0451-4

First edition 2007
Seventh edition 2014

British Library Cataloguing-in-Publication Data
A catalogue record for this book has been applied for from the British Library

Printed in the United Kingdom by Polestar Wheatons

Polestar Wheatons
Hennock Road
Marsh Barton
Exeter
EX2 8RP

Your learning materials are printed on paper obtained from traceable
sustainable sources.

Contents

Question Bank

Your exam will consist of 50 questions worth 2 marks each, together adding up to 100 marks. You should complete them all.

The questions are of three types:

- **Multiple choice** – select 1 from 4 options A, B, C, or D (see Chapter 1 Q2)

- **Multiple response** – select 2 or 3 from 4 or more options (see Chapter 1 Q1)

- **Multi-part multiple choice:** select 1 from 2 or 3 options, for two or more question parts (see Chapter 1 Q5)

Chapter 1: Introduction to business

1   Organisations can be defined or described in various ways. Which THREE of the following are the
    key characteristics that are shared by all organisations?

    A   Synergy

     B   Social arrangement

    C   Collective goals

    D   Specialisation

     E   Controlled performance

     F   Exchange of goods and services

                                                                                        LO 1a

2   What are the primary objectives of profit-oriented and non-profit oriented organisations?

	Profit-oriented organisation	*Non-profit oriented organisation*
A	Output of goods/services	Minimise costs
B	Output of goods/services	Provision of goods/services
C	Maximisation of wealth	Minimise costs
D	Maximisation of wealth	Provision of goods/services

                                                                                        LO 1a

3   At the recent annual general meeting of Vortex plc, a major shareholder voiced his opinion that the
    company was suffering from the symptoms of 'satisficing'. In the context of corporate objectives,
    'satisficing' means that:

    A   Managers seek to make satisfactory profits rather than maximise wealth

    B   Managers seek to keep all stakeholders satisfied

    C   Owners seek to meet a satisfactory level of corporate social responsibility obligations

    D   Owners seek to make satisfactory profits

                                                                                        LO 1a

4   Joe Bright, the managing director of Gargoyle Ltd, has set a primary objective of growth in profits for the company. He aims to concentrate on product development to support this objective. Identify whether the following will be suitable secondary objectives to achieve the growth in profits via product development.

Bringing in new products

 A   Suitable

B   Not suitable

Reducing labour turnover

C   Suitable

 D   Not suitable

Investing in research and development

E   Suitable

F   Not suitable

LO 1a

5   Maximising the wealth of its shareholders is the stated goal of Avernanche plc. The company's objectives have been expressed as a hierarchy of primary and secondary objectives. Identify which of the following is most likely to be the primary business objective.

A   To increase the annual profit after tax by 125% in the next 10 years

B   To introduce an average of two new products each year for the next six years

C   To double the share price within the next 10 years

D   To become the market leader in four market segments within the next 10 years

LO 1a

6   In the opinion of a group of major shareholders, during the past three years the directors of Barrington plc have run the company in a way that has been designed solely to increase their prestige in the business community. According to Baumol, this characteristic of the company is most likely to be evident in the directors' aim to:

A   Maximise wealth

B   Maximise sales revenue

C   Minimise costs

D   Minimise social impact

LO 1a

7   In order to establish whether a particular organisation should be classified as a business or not, it would be necessary to enquire as to the nature of its:

A   Primary objective

B   Mission

C   Vision

D   Secondary objective

LO 1a, 1b

8   The primary objective of ABC Car Rental Ltd is as follows: 'We aim to become the fastest growing company with the highest profit margin in the global vehicle rental and leasing business'.

One of the secondary objectives management has set to achieve this goal is: 'To increase our market share for global family car rentals to 20% within three years'.

Which THREE components of the company's secondary objective are represented in the SMART acronym?

A   S

B   M

C   A

D   R

E   T

LO 1a

9   For a business, which TWO of the following would be classified as secondary objectives?

A   The business's market share target for next year

B   The business's productivity improvement target for next year

C   The business's mission statement

D   The business's financial objective of shareholder wealth maximisation

E   The business's vision

LO 1a, 1b

10   A major airline, FlotAir plc, has been drawing up a mission statement. Which THREE of the following items would you expect to see in it?

A   We will double profits in three years

B   We will encourage diversity in the workplace

C   We intend to be the best airline in the world

D   We aim to give excellent customer service

E   We intend to take over Lufthansa

F   We intend to have a 30% market share on the London to New York route

LO 1a, 1b

11 Two of Sunshine Tours plc's stakeholder groups are putting the company under pressure to improve its return on investment. These are most likely to comprise which TWO of the following groups?

A Shareholders

B Customers

C Bankers

D Suppliers

E Employees

LO 1a, 6e

12 Cruciform is a charity providing medical services in remote rural areas of South America. The chief executive is currently involved in preparing a brochure outlining the services provided by the charity. In that document the chief executive hopes to stress that the charity sees itself being the largest global provider of charitable medical services by 20X5. In highlighting this, the chief executive is stressing the charity's:

A Vision

B Mission

C Primary objective

D Secondary objective

LO 1a, 1b

13 The directors of Gordon Ltd have recently appointed two members of staff to an internal committee that provides suggestions to the company's main board of directors concerning all aspects of the company's strategies and policies.

This decision is an illustration of the company's concern for which major stakeholder?

A Lenders

B Suppliers

C Customers

D Trade unions

LO 1a, 6e

14 Mandrake plc is a large group which processes waste for local authorities. It has stated that it seeks to provide

'our shareholders with increased value, our customers with value for money, our employees with secure and interesting jobs and the public with safe and environmentally sustainable waste disposal.'

This is analysed below into four statements. Identify which ONE is Mandrake plc's primary business objective.

A To provide our shareholders with increased value

B To provide our customers with value for money

C To provide our employees with secure and interesting jobs

D To provide the public with safe and environmentally sustainable waste disposal

LO 1a

15 The ability to meet the needs of the present without compromising the ability of future generations to meet their own needs is known as:

A   Corporate responsibility

B   Sustainability

C   Business ethics

D   Reversability

LO 5g

Business and Finance: Question Bank

1   Hu Song works for Premidian plc. His personal stature and credibility and his relationship with owners, employees and customers bring strong support from these quarters for his application to a senior management post. He generates strong feelings of loyalty and commitment among the people that currently work for him and they know that he has great capabilities and should go far in the company.

Hu Song appears to exhibit which kind of power?

A   Legitimate power

B   Referent power

C   Coercive power

D   Expert power

LO 1d

2   A regional lending manager with a major international bank has the authority to lend up to £1m on an unsecured basis to any single corporate customer without reference to the bank's head office. What sort of power is this?

A   Referent power

B   Expert power

C   Legitimate power

D   Reward power

LO 1d

3   Cerise is a manager who can authorise her own travel expenses up to £1,000. Cerise is about to travel abroad on business and has a choice between flying economy class for £350 or flying business class for £1,050. Cerise is an old friend of the company's travel administrator, Malcolm, who arranges bookings. She persuades him to book the business class seat. This is an example of Cerise exercising:

A   Authority without power

B   Power without authority

C   Delegation of authority

D   Power with authority

LO 1d

4   Michael Upton is a senior manager working for Chirac plc. He has decided to delegate completion of an internal report to one of his subordinates. In doing this, Michael is transferring to the subordinate:

A   Authority, responsibility and power

B   Authority, accountability and power

C   Responsibility and authority

D   Power, responsibility and accountability

LO 1d

5   Pamela is a line manager in the accounting department of Holland plc. This means that Pamela has line authority:

A   Over a subordinate down the chain of command

B   To give specialist advice, but not the right to insist the advice is followed

C   Over a project team's function

D   In certain areas over another department

LO 1d

6   Which of the following managers is operating as a functional manager in the situation described?

A   A human resources manager suggesting aptitude tests for managers to use when recruiting

B   An IT manager setting out rules for Internet and e-mail use

C   A manager setting targets for the workforce

D   A product manager asking IT and marketing staff to help with a big product launch

LO 1d

7   Andrew, a manager in Fortwarren plc, has had to re-arrange a staff rota after a staff member fell ill. According to Mintzberg, this would form part of Andrew's:

A   Decisional role

B   Interpersonal role

C   Disseminator role

D   Informational role

LO 1d

8   Charles Foster is a manager at Tordos Ltd. He is talking to a friend and complaining that all he
     seems to do is attend meetings along with other managers in the company and represent his team
     at a variety of conferences and dinners. In terms of Mintzberg's managerial roles, Charles is
     describing his:

     A   Decisional role

     B   Interpersonal role

     C   Disseminator role

     D   Informational role

                                                                                              LO 1d

9   A new project team has recently been established by Tristam plc. Last week a meeting of the
     project team was held at which clear objectives and performance measures were agreed for the
     project in hand. However, at today's weekly progress meeting, there were numerous arguments
     concerning which roles would be undertaken by which members of staff. From this, it is evident
     that the project team is at which stage of group development?

     A   Forming

     B   Storming

     C   Norming

     D   Performing

                                                                                              LO 1d

10   Samp plc's organisational culture has been analysed by a team of management consultants, who
     have told the directors that the culture is outward-looking but controlling. Samp plc is, therefore:

     A   An internal process culture

     B   A rational goal culture

     C   An open systems culture

     D   A human relations culture

                                                                                              LO 1d

11   Malcolm Christopher is a marketing manager with Stone plc. Whilst his marketing director has
     primary responsibility for the company's overall marketing strategies, Malcolm has day-to-day
     responsibility for all aspects of the company's marketing mix. This means that Malcolm will be
     responsible for:

     A   A set of variables that he manages in order to achieve a desired response from the company's
          various target markets

     B   Budgets setting out the volumes to be sold to the company's various target markets

     C   The sets of different features and benefits that are present in the company's range of products

     D   The types of advertising used by a firm to reach and influence its various target markets

                                                                                              LO 1c

12   Pemble Ltd is a company that emphasises its adoption of the marketing orientation. Which of the following statements is most likely to be made by Ian Pemble, its managing director?

    A   Rather than focusing on product development, we offer discounts on our current lines to increase sales

    B   We increase sales by spending money on development of products our customers want

    C   We put all our effort into persuading customers to buy our products as our sales targets are of paramount importance

    D   We aim to increase sales by spending to develop products we think are innovative

LO 1c

13   In terms of authority which of the following is the best description of a staff function?

    A   A situation where a person is entitled to command another

    B   A function that is carried out only at head office

    C   A situation where a person can give advice and guidance to another

    D   A function that is carried out locally only

LO 1d

14   A firm of management consultants is analysing a particular company's organisational behaviour characteristics. In terms of the organisational iceberg, which THREE of the following are classified as covert variables affecting organisational behaviour?

    A   Formal goals

    B   Attitudes

    C   Underlying competencies and skills

    D   Organisation design

    E   Communication patterns

LO 1d

15   Mike Wells is the managing director of Welldean Ltd, a small company specialising in aromatherapy products. He has been reading about the benefits of market segmentation with regard to both competitive strategy and resource allocation, and is looking to apply it to his company. Adoption of market segmentation by the company would mean that:

    A   The company would sell to only one section of the market

    B   The market is broken down into several different sections

    C   The company sees the aromatherapy market as homogeneous

    D   The competitive scope of the company would be narrow

LO 1c

16   Karen is a general manager with Websellers Ltd. The company is restructuring and Karen is trying to persuade the managing director to set up a separate marketing department within the new structure. Which of the following statements that she has made are true?

Marketing is the principal function of the company:

A   True

B   False

All the different business functions should blend to achieve customer satisfaction:

C   True

D   False

A company cannot practise marketing without a marketing department:

E   True

F   False

LO 1c

17   Manton plc has decided to support the launch of its latest product by means of a major television advertising campaign. This is an example of:

A   Pull promotion

B   Push promotion

C   A combination of pull and push promotion

D   Personal selling

LO 1c

18   Alan Noble is a manager with Glasnow Ltd. He always looks for opportunities to praise his subordinates and takes great pleasure in being able to promote staff who perform well. As far as his subordinates are concerned Alan's actions meet their:

A   Self-actualisation needs

B   Status/ego needs

C   Social needs

D   Safety needs

LO 1d

19 Lynnette is a manager with Grin plc. Her staff all agree that she adopts a Theory X style of management. Identify whether each of the following statements reflects her assumptions.

People must be threatened with punishment if the organisation is to meet its objectives:

A   Reflects

B   Does not reflect

The average person avoids responsibility:

C   Reflects

D   Does not reflect

The intellectual potential of the average person is only partially utilised:

E   Reflects

F   Does not reflect

LO 1d

20 Three factors have been identified as affecting the motivation of employees in Ramble plc's accounting department: working conditions; each employee's relationship with Jeff, the manager; and challenging work. Jeff would like to classify the factors according to Herzberg's theory of hygiene factors and motivating factors. Which of the following classifications is correct?

Working conditions

A   Hygiene factor

B   Motivating factor

Relationship with Jeff

C   Hygiene factor

D   Motivating factor

Challenging work

E   Hygiene factor

F   Motivating factor

LO 1d

21 The process by which a market is divided into homogeneous groups of potential customers who may be treated similarly for marketing purposes is called:

A   Market research

B   Marketing orientation

C   Marketing mix

D   Market segmentation

LO 1d

22 Saggy plc is a business which accepts the needs of potential customers as the basis for its operations. Its success is seen as being dependent on developing and marketing products that satisfy those needs. Saggy plc would be described as having:

A   A marketing orientation

B   A sales orientation

C   A product orientation

D   A production orientation

LO 1d

23 The main influences on a business's pricing are:

A   Place, price, promotion and product

B   Volume, variety, variation in demand and visibility

C   Costs, competitors, customers and corporate objectives

D   People, processes and physical evidence

LO 1d

24 Harris plc has a capital-intensive operation, with specialisation of work and well-established systems for getting the work done. Each month its operations manager is required to produce more items than in previous periods. Using the four Vs model Harris plc's operations manager is therefore expected to manage:

A   High volume and high unit costs

B   High volume and low unit costs

C   Low volume and low unit costs

D   Low volume and high unit costs

LO 1d

25 Research into products which have obvious commercial or practical use is called:

A   Market research

B   Pure research

C   Applied research

D   Process research

LO 1d

26 What are the four elements of the procurement mix?

A   Price, product, place, promotion

B   Quantity, quality, price, lead time

C   Volume, variety, variation in demand and visibility

D   Costs, competitors, customers and corporate objectives

LO 1d

Chapter 3: Organisational and business structures

1   The human resources director of Ginger plc wants new recruits in all areas of the company to have a copy of a chart showing its formal organisation structure. Identify whether each of the following statements about the chart is true or false.

The chart will show the degree of decentralisation in Ginger plc.

A   True ✗

B   False ✓

The chart will show the span of control in Ginger plc.

C   True ✓

D   False

The chart will show the scalar chain in Ginger plc.

E   True ✓

F   False

LO 1d

2   Hamid works for a training company, Lan plc, as a lecturer. The company has been established for over 30 years. He specialises in training bankers. In terms of organisational structure, Lan plc has a large operating core within which all the well-qualified lecturing staff are employed. They need to ensure their teaching material is constantly updated so that it reflects the current issues in the complex banking industry, and to ensure that the company's courses remain competitive. The lecturers are supported by a large administrative team who follow set procedures to ensure the smooth delivery of courses. From these details, it is clear that Lan plc has which of the following organisational structures?

A   Entrepreneurial

B   Machine bureaucracy

C   Professional bureaucracy

D   Divisionalised

LO 1d, 2c

3   Which of the following are THREE of Mintzberg's building blocks of an organisation?

A   Support staff

B   Middle line

C   Functional division

D   Scalar chain

E   Ideology

F   Matrix structure

LO 1d, 2c

4   John's job description at Glue Pot plc mentions that his role is part of the company's technostructure. According to Mintzberg, a technostructure:

   A   Ensures that an organisation follows its mission

   B   Provides ancillary services

   C   Standardises work processes

   D   Controls the work of the operating core

LO 1d, 2c

5   Benton plc is a machine bureaucracy. Which of the following characteristics is the company most likely to exhibit?

   A   The technostructure exerts a pull towards standardised processes

   B   The operating core exerts a pull towards standardised skills

   C   The middle line exerts a pull towards fragmentation

   D   The support staff exert a pull towards collaboration

LO 1d, 2c

6   Amy has just joined the finance department of a local hospital. Her early impressions of the organisation are that its management belong to the 'classical school' because of their adherence to the concept of unity of command. This means that in general the management believe that:

   A   A subordinate should receive orders from only one manager

   B   There should be only one manager of each activity

   C   Authority should flow down a single chain of command

   D   Work should be specialised into single tasks

LO 1d, 2c

7   Justin works for Edwinstone plc. He is part of a project team working on developing a construction site in London for the Olympic Games. The team is a matrix structure with employees from many different departments coming together to work on this project.

   Which of the following management principles set out by Fayol does this type of structure necessarily contravene?

   A   Authority and responsibility

   B   Subordination of individual interests

   C   Unity of command

   D   Esprit de corps

LO 1d, 2c

8   The chief executive of Acton plc has recently been discussing problems caused by the centralised nature of the company's decision-making processes, which have led to accusations from staff and some customers that the company is increasingly slow and unresponsive. The chief executive is keen to increase the amount of decentralised decision-making over the next year.

Which THREE of the following are likely to increase the amount of decentralisation that is possible in Acton plc?

A   The company's authoritarian management style

B   The well-skilled workforce

C   The company's large size

D   The slow pace of technological change in the company's markets

E   The effectiveness of communication across the company

LO 1d, 2c

9   Martin Hardie is a human resources manager with Wardman Ltd. He is currently working on a project designed to increase the spans of control of the managers employed by the company's largest subsidiary. He has been asked to identify any factors about the subsidiary that might suggest that increases in spans of control are possible.

Which of the following four factors identified by Martin suggests that increased spans of control are feasible?

A   Subordinates carry out very similar tasks

B   Subordinates are geographically dispersed

C   Frequent, time-consuming problems arise

D   Managers tend to be engaged in large amounts of non-supervisory work

LO 1d, 2c

10 In terms of structure, Platlet plc is a wide, flat organisation. Which THREE of the following characteristics is the company most likely to exhibit?

A   A greater need to delegate

B   Higher administration and overhead costs

C   Many opportunities for promotion

D   Better communication between the strategic apex and operating core

E   Large spans of control

F   Slow decision making

LO 1d, 2c

11 Logical Computing Ltd adopts a wide, flat organisational structure. With which of the following is it likely to encounter problems?

    A   Ensuring enough face-to-face contact takes place between superiors and staff members

    B   High management overhead costs

    C   Internal communication

    D   Superiors not delegating enough work to staff

LO 1d, 2c

12 Which THREE of the following are characteristics of limited companies?

    A   Perpetual succession

    B   Separate legal personality

    C   Financial statements can remain private

    D   Simple withdrawal of capital

    E   The company's liability is limited

    F   Regulation under the Companies Act 2006

LO 2a, 2b

13 Burns and Stalker classified organisations as 'mechanistic' or 'organic'. For each term, which of the following is an appropriate description?

Mechanistic

    A   Commitment to organisation's mission

    B   Network structure of control

    C   Relatively flexible job descriptions

    D   Suitable for slow moving environments

Organic

    E   Insistence on obedience to superior

    F   Hierarchical structure of control

    G   Very precise job descriptions

    H   Suitable for dynamic environments

LO 1d, 2c

14 Protin plc is a modern manufacturing operation. It uses components manufactured by suppliers and sub-contractors all over the world to assemble finished goods to customer specifications in its assembly plant. Operations managers are technically competent and their competence within the area of their expertise is rarely questioned. There is a high degree of specialisation of labour and procedures ensure that, regardless of who carries out tasks, they are executed in the same way each time. From this description of Protin plc, identify whether the following statements about the company are likely to be true or false.

Innovation is suppressed.

A   True

B   False

Employees are concerned with completing the task efficiently, rather than with how the task can be improved upon for the benefit of the organisation.

C   True

D   False

Everyone in the organisation finds it easy to learn from their mistakes.

E   True

F   False

LO 1c, 2c

_____

15 TinTin Ltd is facing a period of rapid change and innovation in its operating markets. According to Burns and Stalker, which THREE of the following should the company seek to adopt in order to be effective in its environment?

A   A Theory X management style

B   A Theory Y management style

C   A wide, flat organisational structure

D   A tall, narrow organisational structure

E   Extensive use of delegation

F   Limited use of delegation

LO 1d, 2c

_____

16 A company wishes to expand abroad and has found three methods of doing this: a group structure, a joint venture and a strategic alliance. Which of the following descriptions best applies to each method of overseas expansion?

Agreeing with a foreign manufacturer of a complementary product to market both products jointly in both countries

A   Group structure

B   Joint venture

C   Strategic alliance

Taking over a distributor in the foreign market

D   Group structure

E   Joint venture

F   Strategic alliance

LO 2a

17 Which of the following business structures necessarily has a legal identity separate from that of its owner(s)?

A   A joint venture between two limited liability companies

B   A general partnership

C   A limited liability partnership

D   A strategic alliance

LO 2a

18 Angela McHugh is a sole trader who currently employs one person. Her business, Markstat, performs statistical analysis for market research companies. Workloads are increasing rapidly and Angela has realised that she now needs to employ three additional people. This will mean that new office premises have to be found and new furniture and equipment purchased. The business operates in a highly competitive sector.

Identify which TWO of the following factors are disadvantages of her current business structure in this context.

A   A floating charge cannot be used to secure borrowing

B   Angela's liability is unlimited

C   The business's liability is unlimited

D   Financial statements do not have to be filed at Companies House

E   The stringent legal rules that apply to the business's constitution

LO 2b

19   RST is a partnership in which profits are shared between R, S and T in the ratio 3:2:1. The partners wish to incorporate by issuing shares in a new company to the partners and the new company is to take over the assets and liabilities of the partnership. There will be no cash movements between the business and the partners, or between the partners. No loan accounts will be created between the business and its shareholders or directors.

Which of the following statements must be true?

A   Shares will be issued in the ratio 3:2:1 to R, S and T

B   Shares will be issued to match the partners' capital

C   Creditors of the business will be in a stronger position after incorporation

D   Dividends will be paid in the ratio 3:2:1 to R, S and T

LO 2a, 2b

20   Romulus Ltd and Remus Ltd have recently agreed to co-operate to exploit the possibilities that both companies have in a particular overseas market. No separate company has been established for this purpose as the companies' chief executives, who have known each other for many years, have agreed matters informally. This arrangement is an example of a:

A   Licensing agreement

B   Joint venture

C   Strategic alliance

D   Group structure

LO 2a

21   Rumbert plc is a large group listed in the UK, with a head office in London and strategic business units (SBUs) spread throughout the world. Only overall strategic direction and consolidated financial reporting are provided by London. All SBUs manage their own marketing and operations, and report directly to regional centres which provide all other forms of functional support.

Rumbert Insurance is an SBU operating in South Africa and reporting to the Rumbert Southern Africa regional centre. It is engaged in providing home and car insurance direct to consumers. Identify whether the following areas of functional support would be provided to Rumbert Insurance by the Rumbert Southern Africa regional centre.

Sales management

A   Yes

B   No

Financial reporting for the London Stock Exchange

C   Yes

D   No

Periodic management accounts

E   Yes

F   No

LO 2c

22 Which of the following business structures necessarily has a legal identity separate from that of its owner(s)?

A strategic alliance between a limited company and a limited liability partnership

A   Separate legal identity

B   No separate legal identity

A limited liability partnership

C   Separate legal identity

D   No separate legal identity

A registered company

E   Separate legal identity

F   No separate legal identity

LO 2b

23 Mr Dafinone is a sole trader who works alone, maintaining and repairing IT systems. He works about 60 hours per week. He wants to take on a major new maintenance and repair contract for a local hospital's operating theatre. This will require at least 60 working hours each week. It will be extremely profitable if he can acquire the necessary equipment.

Identify whether the following statements about his sole trader status are true or false.

It prevents him from employing staff to help with the contract

A   True

B   False

It gives him personal liability for any failure of his in relation to the hospital IT system

C   True

D   False

It prevents him from obtaining a loan to obtain the equipment

E   True

F   False

LO 2a, 2b

24 Sextet Partnership comprises six partners who share profits 6:5:4:3:2:1. They are considering incorporation as a limited company, Sextet Ltd. Only the six partners will become shareholders on incorporation.

In relation to Sextet Ltd, which of the following statements is necessarily true?

A   All partners will be equal shareholders in Sextet Ltd

B   If Sextet Ltd wishes to raise new share capital, the number of shareholders may be allowed to rise above six

C   All shareholders will become directors and will have the right to be equally involved in the management of Sextet Ltd

D   If one of the shareholders in Sextet Ltd dies, the company will be dissolved

LO 2b

25 Pliar Ltd is considering a number of options to market a new product with Secateur Ltd's help. Identify the description which best suits the business structure suggested for each option.

Buy Secateur Ltd and market the product through that company

A   Group structure

B   Joint venture

C   Strategic alliance

Form a project team with employees of both Secateur Ltd and Pliar Ltd and market the product through that team

D   Group structure

E   Joint venture

F   Strategic alliance

With Secateur Ltd as equal partner, form Plicateur Ltd and market the product through that company

G   Group structure

H   Joint venture

I   Strategic alliance

LO 2a

Chapter 4: Introduction to business strategy

1   In the home computer market, laptop computers would be an example of a:

    A   Product form

    B   Brand

    C   Product class

    D   Generic product

LO 1d

2   Malcolm Nevin works for Dorchester plc. He has been asked by his manager to undertake an internal analysis of the company as part of a strategic planning review. Which THREE of the following analytical techniques will be useful in this context?

    A   Value chain analysis

    B   Porter's five forces analysis

    C   The BCG Matrix

    D   PESTEL analysis

    E   Analysis of distinctive competences

    F   Ansoff's Matrix

LO 1b

3   Sharma Patel is carrying out a PESTEL analysis for her employers, Decron plc. During her research the ageing of the UK's population has become apparent to Sharma as a potentially important strategic issue for the company. In which section of her analysis should Sharma record this matter?

    A   P

    B   S

    C   T

    D   L

LO 1b

4   The marketing director of Birstall plc is currently formulating whether one of the company's products, which is aimed at a small niche market, should be differentiated from its close competitors, although at this stage she is unsure how such differentiation would be achieved in practice. The decision on whether to differentiate or not is a decision concerning the company's:

    A   Functional strategy

    B   Business strategy

    C   Competitive strategy

    D   Product/market strategy

LO 1b,1e

5   Having entered an overseas market and achieved a reasonably dominant position in just under a year, Cassion plc is pleased to have noticed that the threat of new entrants into the market seems to be relatively low. Which TWO of the following are likely to have contributed towards this situation?

A   High initial capital costs

B   A customer base consisting of a few large customers

C   A highly competitive supplier market

D   The market is for services rather than manufacturing

LO 1b

6   With regard to Porter's Five Forces Analysis and new entrants into a market, which of the following pairs of statements is correct?

	Encourages new entrants	*Erects a barrier to new entrants*
A	High competition	Low capital costs
B	A monopoly supplier of a vital component	High competition
C	One large customer	A monopoly supplier of a vital component
D	Low competition	High capital costs

LO 1b

7   Justin plc has a major stakeholder who in the past has been able to exert considerable influence over the environmental impact of the company's manufacturing operations. Specifically, as a result of one recent campaign orchestrated by this stakeholder, a production facility was temporarily closed down for three weeks. The stakeholder writes regularly to the company's chairman regarding a range of environmental issues surrounding the company.

In terms of Mendelow's Matrix the company would be advised to pursue which of the following strategies in respect of this stakeholder?

A   Keep this stakeholder informed at all times about the company

B   Keep this stakeholder satisfied with regard to the company and its strategies

C   Take minimum effort with regard to this stakeholder as he always complains

D   Treat this stakeholder as a key player when formulating future strategies

LO 1b, 6e

8   Seago plc provides exclusive scuba-diving holidays for people over 60 years of age. In terms of Porter's generic competitive strategies, this represents a strategy of:

A   Differentiation

B   Cost leadership

C   Cost focus

D   Differentiation focus

LO 1c, 1d, 1e

9   Martin Scott, a product manager with Mangrove plc, is currently preparing a report for the
     company's directors in which he will provide an assessment of each of the company's existing
     product lines. In preparing his report, Martin is making use of the BCG Matrix. He has classified
     one particular product, the Pluton, as having a low market share in a high growth market. In the
     conclusion to his report, therefore, we would expect Martin to recommend that, with regard to the
     Pluton, the company should pursue:

     A   Either a hold or a divest strategy

     B   Either a hold or a harvest strategy

     C   Either a build or a harvest strategy

     D   A build strategy

LO 1b, 1e

10   Nextron plc manufactures washing machines and has a 20% share of the UK market. The company
     wants to increase its revenues and has decided to add tumble dryers to its range of products. In
     terms of Ansoff's Matrix, this represents a growth strategy of:

     A   Market penetration

     B   Market development

     C   Product development

     D   Diversification

LO 1b, 1c, 1d

11   The board of directors of Swinson plc are currently considering whether to pursue a new strategy
     in respect of one of their major strategic business units. When evaluating a strategic option in this
     way, the final decision on whether to pursue the strategy or not should be judged against which
     THREE of the following criteria?

     A   A cost of entry test

     B   An acceptability test

     C   A suitability test

     D   A feasibility test

     E   An attractiveness test

     F   A payoffs test

LO 1b

12 The Zulon product is manufactured by Arto plc. The product manager for the Zulon is pleased that its dominant market share has been maintained for over five years, but is concerned that market growth has now almost ceased. The product manager does not believe that the product is worthy of any further significant financial support. In these circumstances and in terms of the BCG Matrix, the product manager should be recommending which of the following strategies?

A Hold

B Harvest

C Divest

D Build

LO 1b, 1e

13 Which of the following statements is true about a product life cycle diagram?

A The life cycle diagram predicts when the decline phase will start

B Sales growth always follows the introduction of a product

C Profits are normally highest during the maturity phase

D The mature phase usually lasts about 10 years

LO 1b

14 Charles Frost is the strategy development director of Langham plc. In formulating strategy recommendations for the board of directors, he always uses Porter's Five Forces Analysis as his fundamental means of analysis as he believes that strategy cannot be effectively formulated without first understanding the nature and structure of the competitive forces within an industry. It is clear from this that Charles adopts:

A An emergent-based view of strategic planning

B A positioning-based view of strategic planning

C A resource-based view of strategic planning

D A gap analysis view of strategic planning

LO 1b

15 Millward Ltd sells garden sheds in the south of England. It has a number of local competitors who regularly use price cuts and other sales promotions to win business. The competitors of Millward Ltd have noticed that in the past Millward Ltd always pursues a policy of responding to price cuts by matching prices and then launching a leafleting campaign to houses in the local area. It appears that, in terms of Kotler's competitor reaction profiles, Millward Ltd is:

A Laid back

B A tiger

C Selective

D Stochastic

LO 1b, 1c, 1d

16   Manson Ltd is looking to pursue a differentiation strategy for its Portex sliding-door product. Which THREE of the following might form part of this strategy?

   A   Action to minimise labour and overhead costs

   B   Action to improve productivity

   C   Improved product features and benefits

   D   Promotion of the Portex brand

   E   Use of higher quality materials in the manufacturing process

   LO 1b, 1e

17   Glenway Ltd is a company that sells package holidays from a chain of retail outlets. Grantham Ltd sells new and used cars from a chain of car dealerships. Glenway Ltd and Grantham Ltd are:

   A   Brand competitors

   B   Industry competitors

   C   Generic competitors

   D   Form competitors

   LO 1b, 1c, 1d

18   Hairdooz Ltd operates a large chain of hairdressing salons. Peter Aldiss, a management consultant, has been asked to undertake a review of the company's activities in providing its services to customers. In terms of Porter's Value Chain, Peter has been asked to focus on the primary activities of the company. Peter will, therefore, be analysing which THREE of the following?

   A   Inbound logistics

   B   Procurement

   C   Firm infrastructure

   D   Marketing and sales

   E   Service

   LO 1b

19   A consultant has told the board of Pineapple plc that the strategic planning process should result in a strategic plan, a business plan and an operational plan. The board is unclear as to what these terms mean.

Identify each plan with its definition.

A plan setting out the markets the business intends to serve, how it will serve each market and what finance is required.

A   Strategic plan

B   Business plan

C   Operational plan

A plan setting out how overall objectives are to be achieved, by specifying what is expected from specific functions, stores and departments.

D   Strategic plan

E   Business plan

F   Operational plan

LO 1f

20   Simian plc operates in the financial services sector. Its marketing director is developing the firm's marketing plan. An external marketing consultant has recommended that the PESTEL framework should be used as part of this process. Which of the following statements correctly describes the reason why the PESTEL framework might prove useful?

A   It will identify Simian plc's strengths and weaknesses

B   It will allow a detailed analysis of the structure of the financial services industry

C   It will act as a detailed checklist to assist in understanding the different influences in Simian plc's environment

D   It will help to identify the relative levels of interest and power of Simian plc's stakeholders

LO 1b

21   Asif plc is a large supermarket chain in the UK which manages all its distribution internally. Each of the 120 stores is a profit centre. As part of its strategy development process, Asif plc has identified the following two strategies. Identify whether these are corporate strategies.

Offering its distribution capability from warehouse to stores as a service to other supermarkets

A   Corporate strategy

B   Not a corporate strategy

Training store staff in the handling of personal safety issues

C   Corporate strategy

D   Not a corporate strategy

LO 1e, 1f

22 The specialist services division of Klaxon plc uses highly-qualified professional staff to provide its government-accredited service to its customers. The division is developing its business plan and is reviewing a five forces analysis that was conducted by a consultant. This identifies that rivalry between the very few providers of the specialist service will soon intensify.

Identify whether the following factors stated in the report indicate increased rivalry among providers or not.

Government subsidies for existing providers are to be removed

A   Indicates increased rivalry

B   Does not indicate increased rivalry

Two key customers of the specialist service are to merge

C   Indicates increased rivalry

D   Does not indicate increased rivalry

LO 1b

---

23 When a business's strategy is based on the matching of its internal resources and competences (strengths and weaknesses) with its environmental conditions (opportunities and threats), according to Mintzberg it sees strategy as:

A   Position

B   Ploy

C   Pattern

D   Perspective

LO 1b

---

24 With respect to an industry's life cycle, during which stage would competition be expected to be most intense?

A   Introduction

B   Growth

C   Maturity

D   Decline

LO 1b

Chapter 5: Introduction to risk management

1   In terms of financial risk, credit risk is:

    A   Economic loss suffered due to the default of a borrower, customer or supplier

    B   Risk of choosing the wrong strategy

    C   Risk that customers do not buy the company's products in the expected quantities

    D   Exposure to potential loss that would result from changes in market prices or rates

LO 1h, 1i

2   A company's financial risk is most likely to increase when there is an increase in the proportion of total costs that are:

    A   Variable costs

    B   Direct costs

    C   Fixed costs

    D   Indirect costs

LO 1h, 1i

3   The strategy director of Milton plc is assessing a particular project that he may recommend to the board of directors. He is concerned, however, about the risk-averse attitude of the board to similar projects in the past. In terms of risk, risk aversion is a measurement of:

    A   The probability of risk arising

    B   Project uncertainty

    C   The impact of risk

    D   Appetite for risk

LO 1h, 1i

4   Which of the following pairs of statements in relation to risk and uncertainty is correct?

    Risk

    A   A lack of information

    B   The inability to predict an outcome

    C   The variation in an outcome

    Uncertainty

    D   The variation in an outcome

    E   A lack of information

    F   The inability to predict an outcome

LO 1h, 1i

5   Norman Ltd is a plastics company that developed a new product for use in the home improvement market. Tests on the product proved successful although in extreme conditions the product was shown to be unexpectedly flammable. After much deliberation the company decided not to launch the product. In response to the risks highlighted in the product tests, this decision is an example of managing risk through:

A   Risk avoidance

B   Risk reduction

C   Risk transfer

D   Risk acceptance

LO 1h, 1i

6   Complete each of the following statements concerning risk attitudes.

A risk seeking attitude means that an investment should not be undertaken if there is an alternative investment offering:

A   A lower risk

B   A higher risk

A risk neutral attitude means an investment should not be undertaken if there is an alternative investment offering:

C   A lower return

D   A higher return

LO 1h, 1i

7   Jenny Smith is a risk manager working for Fortune Ltd. At the present time she is investigating the potential gross risk arising from a recent decision to incorporate lower quality materials into the production process for one of the company's key products. In assessing potential gross risk Jenny needs to take account of the:

A   Level of exposure and probability of occurrence

B   Potential loss and probability of occurrence

C   Potential loss and level of volatility

D   Level of exposure and level of volatility

LO 1h, 1i

8   Smertin and Jones is a small firm providing advice on all aspects of personal finance. Their industry is heavily regulated and being a small firm the costs of regulation can be a heavy burden. In a newspaper article this morning it is predicted that a further area of the firm's business, private medical insurance, may be subjected to brand new regulatory requirements from next year. This possibility is an example of:

A   Business risk

B   Financial risk

C   Event risk

D   Market risk

LO 1h, 1i

ICAEW

9   It is known that a particular project will yield either a profit of £100,000 or a loss of £50,000. The profit will arise with a probability of 0.8 and the loss will arise with a probability of 0.2. The project contains:

A   Uncertainty only

B   Risk only

C   Uncertainty and risk

D   Neither risk nor uncertainty

LO 1h, 1i

10   A risk-minimising investor is faced with the following four investment opportunities. Which TWO of the four investments will the investor possibly choose?

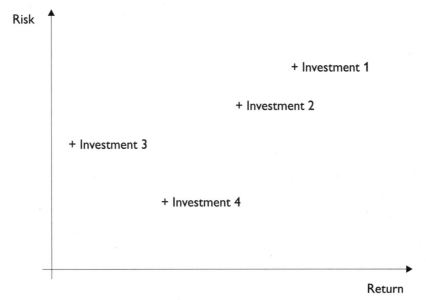

A   Investments 2 and 4

B   Investments 1 and 4

C   Investments 2 and 3

D   Investments 3 and 4

LO 1h, 1i

11   Which of the following is the best definition of the risk concept of 'exposure'?

A   How the factor to which a company is exposed is likely to alter

B   The amount of the loss if the undesired outcome occurs

C   The measure of the way in which a business is faced by risks

D   The likelihood that the undesirable outcome occurs

LO 1h, 1i

12 Which of the following sequences represents the order in which an organisation should respond to risk?

    A   Reduction, avoidance, sharing (or transfer), acceptance (or retention)

    B   Avoidance, reduction, sharing (or transfer), acceptance (or retention)

    C   Reduction, sharing (or transfer), avoidance, acceptance (or retention)

    D   Avoidance, sharing (or transfer), reduction, acceptance (or retention)

LO 1h, 1i

13 Briggs plc has analysed a particular risk faced by its Scarborough division on a risk map. It has concluded that the matter has a low impact but there is a high probability of its occurrence. Which of the following risk responses would be most appropriate?

    A   Risk avoidance

    B   Risk reduction

    C   Risk transfer

    D   Risk acceptance

LO 1h, 1i

14 An organisation responds to an identified risk by restructuring. Which category of control has it used?

    A   Physical controls

    B   System controls

    C   Management controls

    D   Financial controls

LO 1h, 1i

15 Grenville Ltd is renewing its buildings and contents insurance policy covering its eight UK factories. In terms of risk management, this is an example of:

    A   Risk avoidance

    B   Risk reduction

    C   Risk transfer

    D   Risk retention

LO 1h, 1i

16 Process risk, people risk and legal risk are all forms of:

    A   Operational risk

    B   Event risk

    C   Business risk

    D   Strategy risk

LO 1h, 1i

17 For many years, Manley plc's main source of revenue was the sale of 8mm colour films for cameras. This source of revenue has fallen sharply since the development of digital cameras. In relation to the success of digital cameras, Manley plc has been the victim of:

A   Operational risk

B   Event risk

C   Business risk

D   Market risk

LO 1h, 1i

18 A company has recently automated production and this has led to substantial redundancies amongst employees who were paid on an hourly basis (ie variable labour). The company borrowed heavily to finance the purchase of the machinery needed. The effects of these changes on the company's financial risk are that:

A   Both changes (machinery and borrowing) increase the company's financial risk

B   Automation increases financial risk, borrowing decreases it

C   Automation decreases financial risk, borrowing increases it

D   Both changes decrease financial risk

LO 1h, 1i

19 Matrix Ltd, a supplier to Banfield plc, has recently failed to deliver raw materials in line with the terms set down in the supply contract between the two companies. As a result, Banfield plc has had to delay the delivery of products to a major customer. For Banfield plc, the failure of Matrix Ltd to meet its contractual obligations is an example of:

A   Financial risk

B   Product risk

C   Economic risk

D   Event risk

LO 1h, 1i

20 In the risk management process, in which order should the following aspects of risk management proceed?

1   Risk response and control

2   Risk analysis and measurement

3   Risk awareness and identification

4   Risk monitoring and reporting

A   1, 2, 4, 3

B   3, 2, 1, 4

C   2, 3, 1, 4

D   4, 2, 1, 3

LO 1h, 1i

21 Candle plc is concerned about the risk management of its information systems function. The systems director has suggested that information systems management could be wholly outsourced to a third party provider. This action would be a form of:

A   Risk reduction

B   Risk transfer

C   Risk avoidance

D   Risk retention

LO 1h, 1i

22 Identify whether each of the following risks faced by Lump plc should be classified as business risk or non-business risk.

Product risk

A   Business risk

B   Non-business risk

Event risk

C   Business risk

D   Non-business risk

Economic risk

E   Business risk

F   Non-business risk

LO 1h, 1i

Chapter 6: Introduction to financial information

1   Moreton plc produces monthly variance reports for all its production managers, showing the extent and cause of any variances from the company's production plans. These reports enable managers to take corrective action during the following month. In terms of financial information, these reports can be classified as:

A   Planning information

B   Operational information

C   Tactical information

D   Strategic information

LO 3d

2   The area outside an information systems boundary is known as the:

A   Location

B   Setting

C   Context

D   Environment

LO 3d

3   The directors of Royguard plc have recently approved the establishment of an extensive management information system within one of the company's subsidiaries. In arriving at this decision, the directors were likely to have been conscious that the operations of the subsidiary were largely characterised by:

A   Structured decisions

B   Unstructured decisions

C   Non-programmable decisions

D   Non-routine decisions

LO 3d

4 The information systems manager of Detrex plc is keen that all data input into the company's databases should be complete and accurate. As part of his information management role, he makes use of range checks.

The use of range checks should help to deliver:

Completeness

A Yes

B No

Accuracy

C Yes

D No

LO 3d

5 The information systems manager of Hettie plc is keen that all data input into the company's databases should be complete and accurate. As part of his information management role, he makes use of control totals.

The use of control totals should help to deliver:

Completeness

A Yes

B No

Accuracy

C Yes

D No

LO 3d

6 The information systems manager of Ranger plc is keen that all data on the company's databases are the same as their sources and have not been accidentally or deliberately altered, destroyed or disclosed. His concern, therefore is with:

A Data accuracy

B Data integrity

C Data authenticity

D Data completeness

LO 3d

7   The information system employed by Zing plc automatically maintains a log of user activity. This log contains details of identity, log-on and log-off times and details of processing carried out or access attempts made. All transactions are tagged to identify the person responsible for that processing. The log-on details of the user determine processing privileges. Which THREE of the following control objectives should this system effectively address?

A   Prevention

B   Detection

C   Deterrence

D   Correction

E   Accuracy

F   Completeness

LO 3d

8   Which of the following statements concerning systems is correct?

A   A management information system is likely to be the foundation of a transaction processing system

B   Management information systems and transaction processing systems are usually independent

C   Management information systems and transaction processing systems are synonymous

D   A transaction processing system is likely to be the foundation of a management information system

LO 3d

9   Which TWO of the following characteristics relate to strategic information as opposed to operational information?

A   Often based on estimates

B   Often highly aggregated

C   Mostly very accurate

D   Usually routine

LO 3d

10   Which THREE of the following are essential qualities of good information?

A   Detailed

B   Immediate

C   Accurate

D   Profuse

E   User-targeted

F   Complete

LO 3a, 3d

11   A company correctly records and analyses all its sales transactions. At the end of each month a report is produced for the sales director listing details of every sales transaction: customer, products, quantities and prices. Which of the following reflects how the data and information content of this report would be assessed?

Quality of data

A   Good

B   Poor

Quality of information

C   Good

D   Poor

LO 3a, 3d

12   An information system that fails to collect information from its environment will be ignoring information about which THREE of the following?

A   Its transactions

B   Its budgets

C   Competitor action

D   Legislation

E   Its share price

F   Its mission

LO 3a, 3d

13   John Royston is the information systems manager of Alnwick plc. He is currently constructing a system for use by the company including both a 'knowledge base' and an 'inference engine'. It appears, therefore, that John is constructing:

A   A transaction processing system

B   A management information system

C   An expert system

D   A relational database

LO 3d

14   Arkwright Ltd increasingly makes use of the Internet as a source of information to support its decision-making and its strategy formulation. The chief executive, however, is concerned about the company's increasing use of information from the internet as it raises important concerns regarding the information's:

A   Completeness

B   Authority

C   Cost-effectiveness

D   Relevance

LO 3a, 3d

15 The depreciation policies adopted by Gumtree Ltd have remained unchanged for the past five years. According to the *Conceptual Framework for Financial Reporting,* in relation to its financial information this fact supports the qualitative characteristic of:

    A   Understandability

    B   Relevance

    C   Timeliness

    D   Comparability

                                                                                        LO 3a

16 The *Conceptual Framework for Financial Reporting* states that financial information is deemed to be useful when it influences the decisions of users of the information and when it:

    A   Is produced in a timely fashion

    B   Is complete and accurate

    C   Establishes management accountability

    D   Is produced in a cost-beneficial way

                                                                                        LO 3a

17 As a result of reading the financial statements of Tatra plc, Michael Smalley decided to increase his shareholding in the company. In terms of the *Conceptual Framework for Financial Reporting* this appears to confirm that the information in Tatra plc's financial statements was:

    A   Positive

    B   Timely

    C   Material

    D   Relevant

                                                                                        LO 3a

18 Merrick Ltd operates a transaction processing system in which changes in the system can only be made by people who are accountable for them. This aspect of the system contributes towards which one of the essential qualities of a secure information system?

    A   Confidentiality

    B   Integrity

    C   Non-repudiation

    D   Authorisation

                                                                                        LO 3d

19 Each month the Faculty of Business at Newtown University receives financial performance data for the previous month. Each month the senior management of the Business School complain that they cannot rely on this information as every month it contains errors. The information, therefore, is often ignored by managers. In terms of the qualities of a secure information system, the actions of the managers show that the system lacks the quality of:

A   Confidentiality

B   Availability

C   Non-repudiation

D   Authorisation

LO 3d

20 The chief executive of Table plc is discussing the firm's most recent financial statements with his finance director. The chief executive is not convinced about the usefulness of much of the information in the financial statements and, in particular, he identifies three specific characteristics of the information that he feels may undermine its usefulness.

Identify whether these characteristics are likely to undermine the information's usefulness.

Its lack of timeliness

A   Undermines usefulness

B   Does not undermine usefulness

The high level of regulation that applies to it

C   Undermines usefulness

D   Does not undermine usefulness

The high level of aggregation it contains

E   Undermines usefulness

F   Does not undermine usefulness

LO 3a

21 Identify whether the following are key issues in relation to information processing in a company's accounting systems.

Completeness

A   Key

B   Not key

Non-repudiation

C   Key

D   Not key

Verifiability

E   Key

F   Not key

LO 3a, 3d

22 In relation to users of financial information, which of the following statements is true?

    A   External users evaluate the performance of a company's management using management accounting

    B   Financial reporting provides information to managers and people outside the company, such as investors

    C   Management accounting provides information to managers and people outside the company, such as investors

    D   Financial reporting generates confidential information for internal decision makers such as executives and management

                                                                                                    LO 3a

23 According to the *Conceptual Framework for Financial Reporting* to support the effective working of capital markets for the benefit of businesses, financial statements must have which TWO fundamental qualitative characteristics?

    A   Understandability

    B   Relevance

    C   Faithfulness of representation

    D   Comparability

    E   Timeliness

    F   Verifiability

                                                                                                    LO 3a

24 Russell Garnett is an accountant working for Forsell plc. In conversation with a colleague, Russell has made the following points concerning financial statements. Which is true?

    A   Financial statements are used mainly by management

    B   Financial statements are used by parties internal to the business only

    C   Financial statements are used only by investors

    D   Financial statements are used by investors, payables (creditors) and management

                                                                                                 LO 3a, 4b

25 When determining whether information is both of good quality and valuable, the characteristic that it must have is:

    A   Accuracy

    B   Accessibility

    C   Timeliness

    D   Relevance

                                                                                                 LO 3a, 3d

26 An information system which combines data and analytical models or data analysis tools to help with semi-structured and unstructured problem solving of an operational nature is called:

A   An expert support system

B   A decision support system

C   A knowledge work system

D   An office automation system

LO 3d

Chapter 7: The business's finance function

1   Stewardship of the organisation's financial resources is part of which of its finance function's tasks?

   A   Financial reporting

   B   Recording financial transactions

   C   Treasury management

   D   Management accounting

LO 3a, 3b

2   Hamish MacGregor is a finance trainee who has just started working for Bedlam Ltd. The company's finance director has asked Hamish to undertake a capital investment appraisal of a potential project. He has been told to use a capital budgeting technique with discounted cash flow principles.

   Which of the following could Hamish use in appraising the potential project?

   A   Variance analysis

   B   Internal rate of return

   C   Cost-volume-profit analysis

   D   A rolling budget

LO 3f

3   Collinson plc is a medium-sized group operating at four locations in the UK. It operates an entirely centralised finance function but is concerned that the function as a whole is not performing well. In which area is centralisation of the finance function least likely to be effective in this situation?

   A   External reporting

   B   Recording financial transactions

   C   Cash management

   D   Internal reporting

LO 3b, 3c

4   Carrie Swindells has been asked to undertake a capital investment appraisal exercise using only techniques that make allowance for the time value of money. Which of the following investment appraisal techniques could Carrie make use of?

   A   Payback period

   B   Net present value

   C   Return on investment

   D   Return on capital

LO 3b, 3f

5   Which THREE of the following are common purposes of budgets?

A   Guiding managers on how to achieve company objectives

B   Supporting the production of a statement of cash flows

C   Helping to co-ordinate financial reporting activities

D   Allocating finite company resources

E   Communicating a company's plans

LO 1g, 3f

6   Maureen Linacre is employed in the finance function of Gralam plc. Her duties involve ensuring that the company always has sufficient funds available to meet both its short-term and long-term financial requirements. It is clear, therefore, that Maureen is employed by Gralam plc in its:

A   Financial reporting section

B   Management accounting section

C   Treasury management section

D   Transaction processing section

LO 3c

7   Which THREE of the following are characteristics of management accounting information rather than financial reporting information?

A   It is both forward looking and historical

B   It is governed by statute

C   It is primarily used by shareholders

D   It is likely to include a statement of cash flows

E   It is likely to include a cash flow forecast

F   It is likely to include budgetary information

LO 3a

8   The finance function of Bagnall Ltd has been asked to oversee the production of the company's budgets for the forthcoming year. In their initial instructions to the company's various divisions the finance function has stressed that once budgets for next year have been formally agreed steps will be taken to maintain their ongoing relevance by undertaking a monthly review of budgets for forthcoming months in the light of performance in earlier months. It is clear, therefore, that the approach to budgeting adopted by Bagnall Ltd is:

A   Flexible budgeting

B   Incremental budgeting

C   Zero-based budgeting

D   Rolling budgeting

LO 1g, 3f

9 Harold Jemson is an accountant with Farnworth plc. He was recently asked to join a project team looking into the company's compliance with both UK and International Accounting Standards. It appears, therefore, that Harold has been recruited into this project team in order to exploit his expertise in:

A Financial reporting

B Performance measurement

C Capital budgeting

D Strategic management accounting

LO 3c

10 According to the Turnbull guidance on internal control, as part of its assessment of what constitutes a sound system of internal control, managers should look at the extent and categories of:

A Risk which the company regards as excessive

B Uncertainty which the company regards as acceptable

C Risk which the company regards as acceptable

D Uncertainty which the company regards as excessive

LO 3c

11 During the past year Carbon Ltd kept total costs the same, but increased the proportion of fixed costs to variable costs. In these circumstances:

A The profits of the company were less sensitive to changes in sales volume

B The profits of the company were more sensitive to changes in sales volume

C The financial risk of the company decreased

D The company was more profitable

LO 3a

12 Simeon plc is considering the purchase of a new factory. The company's directors have asked its finance function to ensure it uses discounted cash flow principles in its appraisal of the capital investment. The directors always insist upon this because they wish to ensure that in making investments the company is maximising:

A The present value of present cash flows

B The future value of present cash flows

C The present value of future cash flows

D The future value of future cash flows

LO 3a

13 The finance director of Dentrex plc is in charge of the budgeting process within the company. In his initial instructions to the company's operating units he has stressed that at the end of each budget period all budgets will be subject to revision in the light of actual activity levels before any variance analysis is carried out. It is clear, therefore, that the approach to budgeting adopted by Dentrex plc is:

A   Flexible budgeting

B   Incremental budgeting

C   Zero-based budgeting

D   Rolling budgeting

LO 1g, 3a

14 The time value of money is a matter to be considered in which of the following activities undertaken by the finance function?

A   Capital investment appraisal

B   Capital budgeting

C   Pricing

D   Forecasting

LO 3b

15 Novel plc has been establishing its accounting and finance function. The company has been told that two purposes of published, audited financial statements are to help users to assess how effectively managers are running a business and to make judgements about the likely levels of risk and return in the future.

Which of the following user groups of Novel plc's published, audited financial statements is most likely to use accounting information for these purposes?

A   Community representatives

B   Employees

C   Shareholders

D   Managers

LO 3a

16 When a company's accounting and finance function prepares financial statements in accordance with legal rules and accounting standards, it is engaged in the support activity of:

A   Record-keeping and stewardship

B   Planning and control

C   External reporting

D   Internal reporting

LO 3c

17 Mainstream Ltd's finance director wants to establish an effective system in the accounting and finance function for producing management accounting reports. In establishing such a reporting system, which of the following issues should be the finance director's primary consideration?

A   The information needs of the company's managers

B   The need for effective internal control mechanisms

C   The need for cost-effectiveness

D   The need for effective information security

LO 3c

18 Tram plc's finance and accounting section wants to provide information to management on the company's balanced scorecard. This role would be undertaken as part of Tram plc's:

A   Statutory audit requirement

B   Financial reporting function

C   Treasury management process

D   Performance measurement system

LO 3c

19 Identify whether the following three areas in a company are encompassed by the maintenance of control and the safeguarding of assets for the benefit of stakeholders, according to the Professional Oversight Board.

Financial management

A   Yes

B   No

Transactions recording

C   Yes

D   No

The role of non-executive directors

E   Yes

F   No

LO 3c

20 Tim Ogube is advising the managing director of Boiled Sweets plc of the advantages of setting standards and targets to specify the levels of performance that underpin the company's control system. Which THREE of the following are the main components of the company's control system?

A   Measurement of actual performance and comparison against targets

B   Identification of deviations from the plan

C   Establishment of standards or targets to express planned performance

D   Follow-up action to correct adverse results or to exploit favourable variances

E   Measurement of ideal performance

F   Devising the plan

LO 1g, 3b

21 'Effectiveness', 'economy' and 'efficiency' are often cited with reference to resource use. Match these terms with the definitions below:

1 – A reduction or containment of costs

2 – Achieving maximum output at minimum cost

3 – The measure of achievement by reference to objectives

A	1 = effectiveness	2 = economy	3 = efficiency
B	1 = economy	2 = efficiency	3 = effectiveness
C	1 = efficiency	2 = effectiveness	3 = economy
D	1 = economy	2 = effectiveness	3 = efficiency

LO 1a, 3b

22 Which of the following statements about critical success factors (CSFs) for a business is true?

A   Low costs will always be a CSF; high sales revenue will always be a CSF

B   Low costs will always be a CSF; high sales revenue will not always be a CSF

C   Low costs will not always be a CSF; high sales revenue will always be a CSF

D   Low costs will not always be a CSF; high sales revenue will not always be a CSF

LO 1a, 3b, 3e

23 Three basic approaches to performance measures are measures of economy, efficiency, and effectiveness. Economy is measured by:

A   The amount of resources used for the tasks that have been achieved

B   The success in achieving goals and targets

C   Team member satisfaction and the motivational climate

D   The success of the team or work group in controlling its costs

LO 3e

24 The primary focus of the users of financial statements differs according to their interests.

The primary focus of suppliers is on:

A   Liquidity

B   Solvency

C   Risk/return

The primary focus of shareholders is on:

D   Liquidity

E   Solvency

F   Risk/return

LO 3a, 3e, 3f

25 Maria Ragoussi has recently joined the finance function of PTN, a small charity, from Uist plc, a large manufacturing organisation with well-developed performance management systems. She has identified three areas of performance that can be measured in an organisation: effectiveness, economy and productivity. She states that at least one of these areas is common to both types of organisation, whatever their objective.

For each area of performance, indicate whether it is likely to be a key feature of measuring the achievement of the organisation's objective for PTN, Uist plc, or both.

Effectiveness

A   PTN

B   Uist plc

C   Both

Economy

D   PTN

E   Uist plc

F   Both

Productivity

G   PTN

H   Uist plc

I   Both

LO 3e, 3f

26 Which aspects of an organisation's performance with respect to sustainability are measured using 'triple bottom line' measures?

A   Economy, effectiveness, efficiency

B   Economic, social, environmental

C   Profitability, liquidity, investment

D   Productivity, activity, profitability

LO 3e

Chapter 8: Business and personal finance

1 Two brothers run a family-owned removals company which is currently facing liquidity problems and needs an injection of funds. From the following list of sources of finance available to the company, identify which would be classified as a source of short-term finance.

A Share capital

B Bank loan

C Factoring

D Commercial mortgage

LO 3h, 3i

2 Shrier plc is trying to decide on its optimal level of current assets. The company's management face a trade-off between:

A Profitability and risk

B Inventory and receivables

C Equity and debt

D Short-term and long-term borrowing

LO 3h

3 There are a number of motives that influence how much a business wishes to hold in cash. When a company holds cash in order to make the payments that are necessary to keep the business going, such as wages, taxes and payments to suppliers, the motive behind this is:

A The transactions motive

B The finance motive

C The precautionary motive

D The speculative motive

LO 3h

4 A company wants to make sure it has access to standby funds but it cannot borrow at short notice. It will be able to meet its needs if:

A It lowers its level of current assets

B It shortens the maturity schedule of financing

C It increases the level of non-current assets

D It lengthens the maturity schedule of financing

LO 3h

5   If a company moves from a defensive working capital policy to an aggressive working capital policy, it should expect:

A   Liquidity to decrease, whereas expected profitability would increase

B   Expected profitability to increase, whereas risk would decrease

C   Liquidity would increase, whereas risk would also increase

D   Risk and profitability to decrease

LO 3h

6   The legal relationship between a bank and its customer can include the bailor/bailee relationship, the mortgagor/mortgagee relationship and the fiduciary relationship.

Identify each of these relationships with its description.

The bank is expected to act with the utmost good faith in its relationship with the customer.

A   Mortgagor/mortgagee

B   Fiduciary

C   Bailor/bailee

The bank asks the customer to secure a loan with a charge over the customer's assets.

D   Mortgagor/mortgagee

E   Fiduciary

F   Bailor/bailee

The bank accepts the customer's property for storage in its safe deposit and undertakes to take reasonable care to safeguard it against loss or damage.

G   Mortgagor/mortgagee

H   Fiduciary

I   Bailor/bailee

LO 3g

7   The directors at Landsaver plc are considering raising long-term finance by issuing shares in the company. They have been informed that the way to do this is 'by accessing the market' but they are not sure what this means.

A market where new securities are bought and sold for the first time is known as:

A   A futures market

B   A secondary capital market

C   A primary capital market

D   A money market

LO 3h

8   Which of the following statements about venture capital is NOT correct?

    A   Venture capital can be used to fund business start-ups

    B   Venture capitalists may realise their investment by selling their shares following flotation on the stock exchange

    C   Venture capitalists would never sit on the board of a company

    D   Venture capitalists normally expect a company's existing owners to bear a substantial part of the risk

LO 3h

9   Any person who brings together providers and users of finance, whether as broker or principal, is known as:

    A   A business angel

    B   A venture capitalist

    C   A merchant banker

    D   A financial intermediary

LO 3h, 3i

10   Of what type of market is the following a definition?

'A short-term wholesale market for securities maturing in one year, such as certificates of deposit, treasury bills and commercial paper.'

    A   Capital market

    B   Stock Exchange

    C   Alternative Investment Market

    D   Money market

LO 3h, 3i

11   Which of the following is NOT an example of an institutional investor?

    A   Bank of England

    B   A pension fund

    C   An insurance company

    D   A unit trust

LO 3h, 3i

12 In which of the following projects would a venture capital organisation be least likely to invest?

A   A business start-up

B   A management buyout

C   Renovation of a production facility

D   Replacement of an existing production line with a process using a new technology

LO 3h, 3i

13 Which of the following forms of new share issues would normally be underwritten?

A   Introduction

B   Offer for sale by tender

C   Placing

D   Rights issue

LO 3i

14 Which of the following may NOT act as financial intermediaries?

A   Government

B   Building societies

C   Pension funds

D   Clearing banks

LO 3h, 3i

15 Which of the following is NOT a method by which a company can obtain a Stock Exchange quotation for its shares?

A   Offer for sale

B   Placing

C   Rights issue

D   Introduction

LO 3i

16 Which of the following is NOT generally a function of financial intermediaries?

A   The provision of investment advice and information

B   Reduction of risk via aggregation of funds

C   Maturity transformation

D   Prudential control

LO 3h, 3i

17   Which one of the following may be regarded as an advantage to shareholders of a company obtaining a quotation on the London Stock Exchange?

    A   Reduced disclosure requirements

    B   Larger dividends can be paid

    C   Shares become more readily marketable

    D   It entitles a company to put 'plc' (that is, public limited company) after its name

                                                                                    LO 3h, 3i

18   Which of the following is NOT a feature of a finance lease?

    A   The lessor is responsible for the maintenance of the asset

    B   The agreement may split the lease term into a primary period and a secondary period

    C   The capital value of the asset must be shown on the lessee's statement of financial position

    D   The leasing company is normally a bank or finance house

                                                                                    LO 3h, 3i, 3l

19   Which of the following is the source of finance which a company can draw upon most easily in practice?

    A   Cash generated from retained earnings

    B   New share issues

    C   Rights issues

    D   Bank borrowings

                                                                                    LO 3h, 3i

20   With regard to an operating lease, which of the following statements is true?

    A   It is only possible to cancel the agreement during the term at significant cost

    B   With this type of agreement a company sells assets to a finance house and the finance house receives regular payments while the company uses the asset

    C   It is a short-term lease that can easily be cancelled

    D   It is a contract for a specified term, normally equal to the expected asset life

                                                                                    LO 3h, 3i

21   Which of the following statements about venture capital is most valid?

    A   Venture capital is a low risk and low return form of finance

    B   Companies listed on major stock exchanges normally use venture capital to raise new finance

    C   Venture capital can be appropriate for a management buyout

    D   Venture capital normally takes the form of debt finance

                                                                                    LO 3h, 3i

22 Which of the following could a company NOT use as a source of short-term credit?

A   Trade credit from suppliers

B   Bank overdraft

C   Factoring of trade debts

D   Mortgage on property

LO 3h, 3i

23 Which of the following statements is NOT a feature of an overdraft facility?

A   Interest is paid on the full facility

B   Legal documentation is minimal in comparison with other types of loan

C   The facility is repayable on demand

D   Assets are not normally required as security

LO 3h, 3i, 3l

24 Of what is the following statement a definition?

'A document issued by a bank on behalf of a customer authorising a person to draw money to a specified amount from its branches or correspondents, usually in another country, when the conditions set out in the document have been met.'

A   Bill of exchange

B   Export guarantee

C   Banker's draft

D   Letter of credit

LO 3j

25 Which of the following services is least likely to be offered by a factoring company to its client?

A   Provision of finance by advancing, say, 80% of invoice value immediately, and the remainder on settlement of the debt by the client's customer

B   Taking over responsibility for administration of the client's sales ledger

C   Deciding what credit limits the client should give customers

D   Taking over responsibility for irrecoverable debts

LO 3h, 3i

26 KEN plc is awaiting the go-ahead to start its new building programme. This is likely to take place within the next 90 days, but the precise start date and timing of the cash flows are still uncertain. The company has £150,000 available in cash in anticipation of the investment. Which of the following is the least appropriate use of the funds in the interim period?

A   Investment in equities

B   Treasury bills

C   Bank deposits

D   Local authority deposits

LO 3h, 3i

27 In general, for a couple in their 50s with grown-up children their key objective will be to maximise income:

A   As their expenditure is so high

B   So they can save and invest for retirement

C   So they can launch their careers

D   So they can buy their first house

LO 3k

28 An individual has a short- to medium-term financial objective and money to invest in respect of this. Which of the following statements about priority and related risk and return is true in this case?

A   If it is a high priority the individual will want high risk and high return

B   If it is a low priority the individual will want low risk and would accept low return

C   If it is a high priority the individual will want low risk and would accept low return

D   If it is a low priority the individual will not bother to invest

LO 3l

29 Which of the following is NOT a source of finance for households?

A   Bank overdraft

B   Credit cards

C   Commercial paper

D   Hire purchase

LO 3l

30 Financial instruments with maturities of less than one year are traded in the:

A   Equity market

B   Capital market

C   Money market

D   Fixed-income market

LO 3h

31 A 30-year Treasury bond that was issued in the last year is sold in a:

(i)   Money market

(ii) Capital market

(iii) Primary market

(iv) Secondary market

A   Both (i) and (iii)

B   Both (i) and (iv)

C   Both (ii) and (iii)

D   Both (ii) and (iv)

LO 3h, 3i

32 Suppose that you have the choice of two investments carrying similar levels of risk, one is short-term and the other is a long-term bond. You would expect the interest on the longer term bond to be:

A   Normally higher

B   Lower

C   Normally the same

D   Impossible to tell

LO 3l

33 Which part of the Bank of England is responsible for the stability and resilience of the UK's financial system as a whole?

A   Financial Conduct Authority

B   Monetary Policy Committee

C   Financial Policy Committee

D   Prudential Regulation Authority

LO 3g

Chapter 9: The professional accountant

1   The objective of the accountancy profession can best be described as:

    A   Providing financial information about an entity to external users, which is useful to them in making economic decisions and for assessing the stewardship of the entity's management

    B   Measurement, disclosure or provision of assurance about financial information that helps managers, investors, tax authorities and other decision makers make resource allocation decisions

    C   Identifying, measuring, accumulating, analysing, preparing, interpreting and communicating information used by management to plan, evaluate and control an entity and to assure appropriate use of and accountability for its resources

    D   Managing all the processes associated with the raising and use of financial resources in a business

LO 4a

2   What is the objective of the accrual basis of accounting?

    A   To match cash inflows with cash outflows

    B   To match expenses with revenue earned

    C   To match expenses with cash received in the period

    D   To provide financial information to help investors determine the current cash flows

LO 4b

3   Curtis Bowden is a finance manager with Glitch plc. In a conversation with one of his colleagues he has made the following assertions regarding fundamental accounting principles. Which of his assertions is correct?

    A   The principles must be strictly followed even when an amount is insignificant

    B   When in doubt, understate assets and overstate liabilities

    C   A company can never change accounting policies

    D   The choice of inventory valuation method does not need to be disclosed in the financial statements

LO 4b

4   The professional accountant should always be aware that there are certain accounting principles that underlie accounting, financial reporting and assurance. Identify which accounting principle is at issue in each of the following statements.

It is assumed that the company will continue on long enough to carry out its objectives and commitments, so non-current assets are shown at cost less depreciation.

A   Prudence

B   Going concern

C   Materiality

A very large company's financial statements have the amounts rounded to the nearest £1,000.

D   Prudence

E   Going concern

F   Materiality

LO 4b

5   The accounting principle that states that an item in the financial statements would make a difference if its omission or misstatement would mislead the reader of the financial statements under consideration is:

A   The going concern principle

B   The materiality principle

C   The cost-benefit principle

D   The substance over form principle

LO 4b

6   If accrued revenue was omitted from a company's financial statements, the effect on the company's income statement and statement of financial position would be that:

A   The revenue, retained earnings and current liabilities will be understated

B   The revenue, retained earnings, and current assets will be understated

C   Retained earnings and non-current assets will be understated

D   Current assets will be understated and retained earnings will be overstated

LO 4a

7   The accounting principle that states a company should use the same accounting methods and procedures from one accounting period to the next is:

A   The materiality principle

B   The consistency principle

C   The prudence principle

D   The faithful representation principle

LO 4b

8   There are certain activities carried out by accountants which legislation requires to be carried out by members of certain bodies that are 'recognised professional regulators'. Which THREE of the following activities are included in such requirements?

A   Insolvency

B   Management consultancy

C   Investment business

D   Taxation

E   Payroll

F   Statutory audit

LO 4c

9   Svenson, Garnier and Delaquier (SGD) is a major international firm of chartered accountants. John has just joined the firm after working for a sole practitioner who had to retire due to ill health. His friend, Beth, who has worked for SGD for five years helped him get the job. However, she has just found out that he exaggerated his degree results and his previous work experience on his application form. In which of the following areas has John breached the ICAEW Code of Ethics?

A   Integrity

B   Objectivity

C   Professional competence

D   Confidentiality

LO 4b, 4c

10   The senior partner of a firm of chartered accountants is going from the UK to the Bahamas for two weeks, all expenses paid courtesy of the chairman of a client company. Identify whether the following statements concerning this situation are true or false.

Receiving a benefit in the form of goods, services or hospitality from a client is permissible provided all such receipts are declared, including their origin and value.

A   True

B   False

Hospitality from clients should not be accepted because to accept such gifts threatens objectivity.

C   True

D   False

Although accepting most benefits such as gifts is prohibited, it is perfectly in order to accept this type of hospitality from a client.

E   True

F   False

LO 4b, 4c

11 You work for a firm of chartered accountants. A colleague is leaving and wants to make a good impression at the new firm by bringing in new business. She has asked you to run off a copy of the client list to which you have access so that she can target some likely clients. Breach of which fundamental professional principle in the ICAEW Code of Ethics is she proposing?

A   Integrity

B   Objectivity

C   Professional competence

D   Confidentiality

LO 4b, 4c

12 The five threats to fundamental professional principles are:

A   Self-interest, self-review, encroachment, familiarity and intimidation

B   Self-interest, self-review, advocacy, familiarity and intimidation

C   Self-interest, self-review, advocacy, familiarity and intimacy

D   Self-promotion, self-review, advocacy, familiarity and intimidation

LO 4b, 4c

13 You are a chartered accountant in public practice. A friend and colleague of yours, Jill, has just got engaged to the managing director of Argyle Ltd where she used to work until about a year ago. She started working on their audit six months ago. Identify whether the following statements about this situation are true or false.

An objective attitude towards a client is subject to self-interest or familiarity threats as a consequence of family or other close personal or business relationships.

A   True

B   False

Where a close personal relationship exists between a member and someone in a client organisation, that person can continue to act for the company providing sufficient safeguards are in place.

C   True

D   False

A person should not personally take part in a company audit if they have worked for that company within two years of the period of the audit.

E   True

F   False

LO 4b, 4c

14 Gordon is the audit manager in the audit firm of Dark & Co. Sports Galore Ltd has been an audit client for five years and Gordon has been audit manager for the past three years. He has also just acquired about 5% of Sports Galore Ltd's share capital as an inheritance on the death of a distant relative. Sports Galore Ltd is attempting to obtain a listing on the London Stock Exchange and, as the company's auditor, the management would like Gordon and the audit partner to attend an evening reception in a hotel, where they will present their listing arrangements to banks and existing major shareholders.

Identify whether the following threats apply in relation to this situation.

Self-interest threat

A   Applies

B   Does not apply

Self-review threat

C   Applies

D   Does not apply

Advocacy threat

E   Applies

F   Does not apply

LO 4b, 4c

---

15 Using the accrual basis of accounting, revenue is recorded and reported only when:

A   Goods or services are delivered whether or not cash has been received

B   Cash is received at the time goods or services are delivered

C   Cash is received whether or not goods or services have been delivered

D   Cash is received after goods or services have been delivered

LO 4b

---

16 The ICAEW Code of Ethics exemplifies which of the following theoretical approaches to ethical codes?

A   A rules-based approach

B   A framework-based approach

C   A compliance-based approach

D   A tick box approach

LO 4b

---

17 Part A of the IESBA Code of Ethics is a framework that applies to all professional accountants and it introduces the fundamental principles. In this context 'fundamental' means:

A   That the principles form the bedrock of professional judgements and practice

B   That the principles are the easiest aspects of the professional accountant's work

C   That the Code is compliance-based

D   That adherence to rules is all that is required of a professional accountant

LO 4b

18 The managing director of Wendle Ltd wants to understand the links between technical competence and professional responsibility in the accounting profession. Identify whether he should consider the following areas.

Disciplinary proceedings

A   Yes

B   No

Accounting principles

C   Yes

D   No

The profession's interest

E   Yes

F   No

LO 4b

19 According to the Companies Act 2006, qualification as a chartered accountant and appointment as a director of a company together qualify an individual to be appointed as:

A   Company actuary, if it is an insurance company

B   Company secretary, if it is a listed company

C   Company valuer of investment properties, if it is a property company

D   Company liquidator

LO 4b

20 In relation to the external audit or statutory audit of a limited company in the UK, a colleague has made the following statements. In each case, indicate whether the statement is true or false.

'To act as statutory auditor, the person appointed **must** be a member of a recognised supervisory body.'

A   True

B   False

'To act as statutory auditor, the person appointed **must** be either a body corporate or a partnership.'

C   True

D   False

'To act as statutory auditor, the person appointed **must** hold a recognised qualification obtained in the UK.'

E   True

F   False

LO 4b

21 Xigent plc employs directors of finance, of human resources and of legal services, as well as a company secretary. The company is having operational problems which are delaying its completion of a key project. If the project misses its deadline Xigent plc may suffer heavy penalties under the terms of its sales contract with the customer. Part of the delay has been caused by strikes due to bad industrial relations with both employees and sub-contractors, but Xigent plc is unsure whether the penalties included in the contract will come into effect given this reason.

Identifying whether the penalties are likely to come into effect is the role of Xigent plc's:

A   Director of finance

B   Director of human resources

C   Director of legal services

D   Company secretary

LO 4c

22 Part A of the ICAEW Code of Ethics establishes the fundamental principles of professional ethics for professional accountants and provides a conceptual framework for applying those principles.

Which THREE of the following are stated as fundamental principles in the ICAEW Code of Ethics?

A   Integrity

B   Independence

C   Confidentiality

D   Objectivity

E   Reliability

LO 5g

Chapter 10: Structure and regulation of the accountancy profession

1 Luton & Co, a firm of chartered accountants, has recently been offered a consent order by the ICAEW's Investigation Committee. This means that:

    A   The firm could be excluded from membership of the ICAEW

    B   The firm's practising certificate could be suspended

    C   There is a case to answer but it is not so serious as to warrant either exclusion from membership of the ICAEW or suspension of the firm's practising certificate

    D   There would be less publicity than under an order issued by the Disciplinary Committee

LO 4c

2 The ICAEW's Professional Standards Department is responsible for implementing the ICAEW's disciplinary procedures, including the handling of complaints against members. However, the complaint against Roche & Co about an audit it has performed , which has just been brought to the Department's attention, is already in the public domain and is so serious that it might affect the reputation of the accountancy profession in general. In such circumstances, the Department may refer the matter straight to:

    A   The FRC's professional discipline team within its Conduct Division, running the Accountancy Scheme

    B   The FRC's professional oversight team within its Conduct Division

    C   The FRC's audit quality review team within its Conduct Division

    D   The Financial Conduct Authority

LO 4c

3 Tom Laing, a chartered accountant, has recently been the subject of a complaint by one of his clients. The initial stage of the ICAEW's complaints and disciplinary procedure will involve trying to find a practical solution such as giving an explanation or providing information to solve the problem. This stage of the process is referred to as:

    A   Consideration

    B   Arbitration

    C   Investigation

    D   Conciliation

LO 4c

4   The ICAEW's Investigation Committee has recently looked into a complaint brought by a client against Denton & Co, a firm of chartered accountants. The Investigation Committee has found that there is a case to answer and has offered an unpublicised caution to the firm. The firm does not, however, agree that there is a case to answer. In such circumstances, Denton & Co have a right to ask that the case be considered by the:

A   Appeal Committee

B   Disciplinary Committee

C   The Financial Reporting Council

D   The Prudential Regulation Authority

LO 4c

5   Paula Church recently established her own accountancy practice from small retail premises in Hightown. For the time being she will operate as a sole trader. Paula passed the last of her professional examinations last month although she is not yet qualified to offer statutory audit, insolvency or investment business services. She has already been successful in attracting a number of clients to her new practice but she has not yet registered with one of the Consultative Committee of Accountancy Bodies (CCAB). As a result, which of the following statements is correct?

A   She cannot call herself an accountant

B   The CCAB can legally stop her from practising

C   She can offer the full range of accountancy services

D   She can offer the full range of accountancy services except in the reserved areas

LO 4c

6   In relation to which of the following does the Financial Reporting Council have statutory powers?

A   The supervision of the auditing profession by the recognised supervisory bodies

B   Professional discipline

C   Registration within the accountancy profession

D   Continuing professional education and development

LO 4c

7   In addition to its functions in relation to audit and accountancy, the Financial Reporting Council also oversees regulation of:

A   The actuarial profession

B   The insolvency profession

C   The financial advisory profession

D   The investment management profession

LO 4c

8   Kath Parker is considering training as an accountant and she has noticed that there are currently a number of pathways to ICAEW membership, one of which is joining as a CCAB member. Regarding the CCAB, identify whether each of the following statements is true or false.

The CCAB has five members.

A   True

B   False

The CCAB provides a forum in which matters affecting the profession as a whole can be discussed and co-ordinated and it enables the profession to speak with a unified voice to government.

C   True

D   False

LO 4c

9   Through its IESBA Code of Ethics, the International Federation of Accountants (IFAC) encourages accountants worldwide to adhere to five core professional principles.

Identify whether the following are among those principles.

Expertise

A   Yes

B   No

Confidentiality

C   Yes

D   No

Reliability

E   Yes

F   No

LO 4b

10   Chris Prentice runs his own printing company. He is currently experiencing financial difficulties and some of his credit suppliers are threatening to take him to court. He needs some advice and has seen an advertisement in his local paper for an accountancy service that is much cheaper than he expected. He calls the accountant to check that it is not a misprint and is surprised at some of the answers he is given to his questions.

Are the following statements made by the accountant correct or not?

Anyone is free to advertise as an 'accountant' and offer the full range of accountancy services, with no exceptions.

A   Yes

B   No

ICAEW members are open to competition from anyone, whether professionally qualified or not, who chooses to enter the market.

C   Yes

D   No

There is no legal requirement for an accountant to be a paid-up member of one of the CCAB bodies.

E   Yes

F   No

LO 4c

11   Identify whether each of the following statements concerning methods of regulating the accountancy profession is true or false.

In relation to its members, the ICAEW has direct responsibility for:

Dealing with professional misconduct by its members

A   True

B   False

Acting as adviser to the government on necessary legislative changes

C   True

D   False

Confirming eligibility for the performance of reserved activities under statutory powers delegated by the government

E   True

F   False

LO 4c

12   The Financial Reporting Council consists of:

A   Two divisions – the Conduct Division and the Codes and Standards Division

B   Two divisions – the Accountancy Division and the Actuarial Division

C   Three divisions – the Audit Regulation Division, the Accountancy Oversight Division and the Professional Discipline Division

D   Three divisions – the Conduct Division, the Codes Division and the Standards Division

LO 4c

13 Identify whether each of the following statements about the purpose of regulating professions is true or false.

Regulation of professions should:

Protect the public from being misled or from suffering from abuse of power through knowledge or monopoly

A   True

B   False

Ensure that technical, educational and ethical standards are maintained at a level the public has a right to expect

C   True

D   False

Protect vested interests from competition so as to maintain public confidence that the public interest is being safeguarded

E   True

F   False

LO 4c

14 The following statements concern the role of the Disciplinary Tribunal convened by the FRC under the Accountancy Scheme. Identify whether each statement is true or false.

To ensure their independence, no member of a Tribunal can be an officer or employee of any of the accountants' professional bodies, or the FRC.

A   True

B   False

Tribunal hearings are not normally open to the public, except in exceptional circumstances where the Tribunal decides that this would be in the interests of justice.

C   True

D   False

LO 4b, 4c

15 The following statements concern the role of the FRC's Disciplinary Tribunal. Identify whether each statement is true or false.

A Tribunal hearing is less formal than court proceedings but is subject to the same restrictions as a court might have in accepting evidence.

A   True

B   False

The accountant or firm which is the subject of the complaint is entitled to attend and be legally represented at the hearings and will have a full opportunity to defend any complaints, present evidence and challenge any evidence against them.

C   True

D   False

LO 4b, 4c

16   Raymond & Co, a firm of chartered accountants, is currently the subject of the ICAEW disciplinary procedure. If the Disciplinary Committee decides that a penalty should be imposed on the firm, it has the power:

To fine the firm

A   Yes

B   No

To exclude the firm from membership of the ICAEW

C   Yes

D   No

To offer an unpublicised caution

E   Yes

F   No

To take away a member's practising certificate

G   Yes

H   No

LO 4b, 4c

17   The Professional Standards Department of the ICAEW is responsible for implementing the ICAEW's disciplinary procedures, including the handling of complaints against members. Complaints are usually that a member or firm:

Has departed from guidance

A   Yes

B   No

Has brought the ICAEW, the profession or themselves into disrepute

C   Yes

D   No

Is in breach of a principle

E   Yes

F   No

LO 4b, 4c

18   The recent financial statements of Anson plc, a company listed on the London Stock Exchange, depart from the requirements of certain relevant accounting standards and provisions of the Companies Act 2006. The company is therefore likely to be referred to which of the following regulatory bodies?

A   The Prudential Regulation Authority

B   The Financial Conduct Authority

C   The Institute of Chartered Accountants in England and Wales

D   The Financial Reporting Council

LO 4c

19   The Finance Director of Trun plc is a chartered accountant. She has received notice that, in respect of Trun plc's financial statements, she could be subject to disciplinary proceedings by the Professional Standards Department of the ICAEW, or by the Financial Reporting Council's professional discipline team. The latter will only be involved if the matter raises issues affecting:

A   The public interest

B   The independence of the auditors

C   Corporate governance

D   International accounting standards

LO 4c

Chapter 11: Governance, corporate responsibility, sustainability and ethics

1   Which THREE of the following attributes are identified by Phillipa Foster Back as being typical of ethical business leaders?

    A   Fair mindedness

    B   Honesty

    C   Ability to listen

    D   Empathy

    E   Accountability

LO 5g

2   The USA is often referred to as being a market-based financial system. Consequently, its financial system will be characterised by:

    A   Comparatively more government regulation than a bank-based system

    B   Comparatively less close relationships between banks and businesses than in a bank-based system

    C   Comparatively more risk averse households than in a bank-based system

    D   Households with less access to investment in physical assets than in a bank-based system

LO 5d

3   In the country of Zanadu, the population has a risk seeking attitude towards financial matters. Zanadu's financial system is likely to be:

    A   A market-based system

    B   A stakeholder system

    C   A bank-based system

    D   A public policy system

LO 5d

4   Under the UK's unitary board structure, a company's board of directors is responsible for both management of the business and reporting to:

    A   The non-executive directors

    B   The supervisory board

    C   The company's employees

    D   The company's shareholders

LO 5d

5   In both bank-based and market-based financial systems, financial intermediation is of increasing importance due to its ability to address the market imperfection of:

A   Monopoly

B   Asymmetric information

C   Trade barriers

D   Tariffs and quotas

LO 5d

6   The agency problem is a driving force behind the growing importance attached to sound corporate governance. In this context, the 'principal' is:

A   The body of customers

B   The body of shareholders

C   The body of managers

D   The company

LO 5a

7   Identify whether each of the following statements matches the definition of corporate governance set out in the OECD's *Principles of Corporate Governance*.

The practices and procedures for trying to ensure that a company is run in such a way that it achieves its objectives.

A   Matches

B   Does not match

A set of relationships between a company's management, its board, its shareholders and other stakeholders.

C   Matches

D   Does not match

LO 5a

8   The directors of Clamin plc state in the company's annual report that their adherence to the requirements of the UK Corporate Governance Code is driven by their belief that the aim of corporate governance is the nurturing of enterprise while ensuring accountability in the exercise of power and the patronage of firms. It is clear from this that the directors of Clamin plc have adopted:

A   The corporate perspective on corporate governance

B   The public policy perspective on corporate governance

C   The legal perspective on corporate governance

D   The stakeholder perspective on corporate governance

LO 5a

9   Different corporate governance systems have emerged across the world reflecting the different systems by which companies are managed and controlled. These management differences are often reflected in different board structures. Identify whether each of the following statements about the structure of a board of directors is true or false.

In the UK and Germany there is a unitary board of directors system.

A   True

B   False

A two-tier system comprises a management board and a supervisory board.

C   True

D   False

The management board has powers to approve or not approve the financial statements and dividends declared.

E   True

F   False

LO 5d

10   Which of the following is one of the five OECD *Principles of Corporate Governance*?

A   Promote transparent and efficient financial reporting

B   Recognise the rights of stakeholders

C   The equitable treatment of major shareholders

D   Real time, accurate disclosure

LO 5a

11   Identify whether each of the following statements regarding ethics and social responsibility is true or false.

An ethical audit is a process which measures both the internal and external consistency of a company's values base.

A   True

B   False

How far an organisation protects stakeholders with which it has contractual relationships is a measure of its social responsibility.

C   True

D   False

LO 5g

12　The principal factor moulding the nature of business ethics over time is

　　A　The expectations of society

　　B　The values of senior management

　　C　Company policies

　　D　Government regulation

LO 5g

13　Carol Narey has arranged a meeting with a local journalist to advise him about practices at her employer's premises that she believes breach strict government regulations on health and safety issues. She is aware of the risks involved in taking this course of action, although she should also be aware that in such circumstances she would be protected by:

　　A　The Freedom of Information Act

　　B　The Human Rights Act

　　C　The Public Interest Disclosure Act

　　D　The Data Protection Act

LO 5g

14　A financial system comprises which THREE of the following?

　　A　Governance structures

　　B　Intermediaries

　　C　Securities

　　D　Markets

　　E　Regulators

LO 5d

15　The ability of markets to allocate resources efficiently within a financial system is often impeded by the existence of market imperfections. Which THREE of the following are market imperfections regularly associated with financial markets?

　　A　Lack of codes of practice

　　B　Information asymmetry

　　C　Transaction costs

　　D　Lack of regulation

　　E　Insider dealing

LO 5d, 6b

16 The body responsible for promoting high standards of corporate governance in the UK is the:

A   FRC

B   OECD

C   CCAB

D   Bank of England

LO 5b, 5d

17 Woolmer plc adopts social responsibility as a key element in its strategies. This will mean that the company:

A   Seeks to meet the minimum obligations it owes to stakeholders

B   Seeks to exceed the minimum obligations it owes to stakeholders

C   Seeks to meet the minimum obligations it owes to shareholders

D   Seeks to exceed the minimum obligations it owes to shareholders

LO 5b

18 In seeking to address the problem of the separation of ownership and control, corporate governance attempts to align the interests of which TWO of the following stakeholders?

A   Investors

B   Employees

C   Regulators

D   Managers

E   Auditors

LO 5b

19 The stewardship approach to corporate governance requires directors of limited companies:

A   To act at all times in the best interests of the company

B   To allow shareholders to see detailed accounting records upon request

C   To hold regular monthly meetings to answer shareholders' questions

D   To consult the shareholders over difficult management decisions

LO 5a

Chapter 12: Corporate governance

1   Jacob Manning has just been appointed as a non-executive director of Pulsemania Ltd. He needs to know for which of the following matters he is responsible as a non-executive director.

Satisfying himself on the integrity of the company's financial information

A   Responsible

B   Not responsible

Reporting on the performance of the company

C   Responsible

D   Not responsible

Determining appropriate levels of remuneration for executive directors

E   Responsible

F   Not responsible

Satisfying himself that financial controls and systems of risk management are robust and defensible

G   Responsible

H   Not responsible

LO 5c, 5e

---

2   The board of directors of Raygold plc are considering the balance of the company's board. In particular, the company's chairman is considering which of the company's non-executive directors can be classified as independent. Even if a non-executive director has worked as an employee for the company in the past, he/she may still be classified as independent if the period of employment finished at least

A   Two years ago

B   Three years ago

C   Four years ago

D   Five years ago

LO 5c, 5e

---

3   Jumpers plc has just joined the FTSE 350. Identify whether each of the following statements is true or false.

Being outside the FTSE 100, the UK Corporate Governance Code does not apply to Jumpers plc.

A   True

B   False

Being in the FTSE 350, the UK Corporate Governance Code does apply to Jumpers plc and it must not depart from any of its requirements.

C   True

D   False

LO 5c, 5e

Chapter 12: Corporate governance   87

4   John Hammond is an executive director of Underwood plc. Under the terms of the UK Corporate Governance Code, performance-related elements of his remuneration:

A   Must be declared in the company's financial statements

B   Must be a significant proportion of his total remuneration package

C   Are not recommended for him

D   Must be subject to annual review by the company's non-executive directors

LO 5c, 5e

5   A company may seek to improve corporate governance by ensuring that:

A   The chairman and chief executive are the same individual in order to avoid confusion over who has responsibility for running the company

B   The chairman and chief executive are different individuals in order to prevent one person having too much power within the company

C   The chairman and chief executive are different individuals in case one dies or becomes incapacitated due to ill health

D   The company chairman does not take up outside directorships

LO 5c, 5e

6   The performance of Petula Groves in her role as an executive director of Jemson plc for the past year is due to be evaluated in line with the requirements of the UK Corporate Governance Code. This means that her performance will be judged in terms of:

A   Her effectiveness of contribution and time commitment to the role

B   Her time commitment to the role only

C   Her effectiveness of contribution only

D   Neither of these

LO 5c, 5e

7   The UK Corporate Governance Code proposes principles for the level and make-up of directors' remuneration. Which of the following form part of those principles?

Link remuneration to corporate and individual performance

A   Yes

B   No

Establish a formal and transparent procedure for developing policy on executive remuneration and for fixing the remuneration packages of individual directors

C   Yes

D   No

Obtain the auditor's approval of the remuneration set

E   Yes

F   No

LO 5c, 5e

8　The board of directors of Kempton plc is currently considering the membership of its remuneration committee. In this regard, which of the following statements is true?

A　The chairman must be one of the members of the remuneration committee

B　The chairman may be both a member and chair of the remuneration committee

C　The chairman may be a member but cannot chair the remuneration committee

D　The chairman cannot be a member of the remuneration committee

LO 5c, 5e

9　Identify whether each of the following statements concerning corporate governance is true or false.

Non-executive directors of FTSE 350 companies, once appointed, only need to be submitted for re-election every three years

A　True

B　False

The board's responsibility to present a fair, balanced and understandable assessment of company performance extends not only to annual financial statements but also to interim reports

C　True

D　False

The UK Corporate Governance Code states that directors' service contracts should not exceed three years

E　True

F　False

LO 5c, 5e

10　Flange plc is planning its forthcoming annual general meeting. As part of this process the chairman of the company should arrange for which of the following committees to be represented by their chairman at the meeting?

A　Audit

B　Audit and Remuneration

C　Audit, Remuneration and Nomination

D　None of these

LO 5c, 5e, 5f

11 Paul Anson has become aware of theft from his company, Mortice plc, by one of its directors. He wishes to bring this to the attention of the company but is not aware of how best to go about this. Under the UK Corporate Governance Code, who within a company is responsible for reviewing arrangements by which staff may, in confidence, bring matters such as this to the attention of the company?

A   The company chairman

B   The board of directors

C   The non-executive directors

D   The audit committee

LO 5c, 5e, 5f

12 Merton plc is a small listed company outside the FTSE 350. As a consequence, the company:

A   Must comply with all the requirements of the UK Corporate Governance Code

B   Is governed by other corporate governance regulations than the UK Corporate Governance Code

C   Can be flexible in how it applies the UK Corporate Governance Code

D   Is not affected by the requirements of the UK Corporate Governance Code

LO 5c, 5e

13 On which of the fundamental accounting principles are the directors of a company expected to report in the company's annual financial statements?

A   The going concern status of the company

B   The materiality of specific transactions

C   The accrual approach to accounting

D   The consistency of treatment of particular items or transactions

LO 5c, 5e

14 Slaithwaite plc is a small listed company outside the FTSE 350. This means that, according to the UK Corporate Governance Code, the minimum number of independent non-executive directors that should sit on the company's board is:

A   One

B   Two

C   Three

D   Variable as it depends on the total number of people on the board

LO 5c, 5e

15 Shareholders often believe the external (or statutory) auditor's opinion means that the financial statements of a company are 'correct'. If the published financial statements are subsequently found to be 'incorrect', perhaps due to a fraud, shareholders then blame the auditor, but responsibility for preventing and detecting fraud and error lie with:

A   The directors of the company only

B   The directors and management of the company

C   The management of the company only

D   The company's audit committee

LO 5c, 5e, 5f

16 Hilditch plc is currently drawing up a shortlist of potential members of its audit committee. Under the UK Corporate Governance Code, the shortlist must comprise only:

A   Independent non-executive directors with recent and relevant financial experience

B   Independent non-executive directors with at least one who has recent and relevant financial experience

C   Non-executive directors with recent and relevant financial experience

D   Non-executive directors with at least one who has recent and relevant financial experience

LO 5c, 5e, 5f

17 Leopold plc is considering the company's systems of risk management and internal control. Under the requirements of the UK Corporate Governance Code, who is responsible for maintenance of sound risk management and internal control systems?

A   Just the executive directors

B   Just the non-executive directors

C   The entire board of directors

D   The audit committee

LO 5c, 5e, 5f

18 Megan Salisbury is currently full-time executive director of Rifkind plc, a FTSE 100 company. She has been approached by the executive directors of Carnforth plc, another FTSE 100 company, who would like her to take on the role of chairman of Carnforth plc in addition to her existing role with Rifkind plc. In this situation, the guidance provided by the UK Corporate Governance Code means that:

A   Megan should be allowed to accept the offer

B   Megan should not be allowed to accept the offer

C   Megan should only be allowed to accept the offer if she can show she has the available time

D   Megan should only be allowed to accept the offer if the non-executive directors of both companies agree

LO 5c, 5e

19 Cheshunt plc is currently considering the re-appointment of its external (statutory) auditors. The precise level of remuneration to be paid to the external auditors has now been agreed between the company chairman and the senior partners of the audit firm. However, under the requirements of the UK Corporate Governance Code, before matters can be finalised the chairman of Cheshunt plc needs to obtain the approval of:

A   The nomination committee

B   The remuneration committee

C   The board of directors

D   The audit committee

LO 5c, 5e, 5f

20 Sheila Brennan is the chief executive of Forton plc. The company's remuneration committee has recently been putting together a new long-term incentive scheme for Sheila, the details of which have now been agreed. However, under the requirements of the UK Corporate Governance Code, before matters can be finalised the scheme should be approved by the company's:

A   Board of directors

B   Shareholders

C   Chairman

D   Non-executive directors

LO 5c, 5e

21 The UK Corporate Governance Code requires that the percentage of the board of directors of a listed company (excluding the chairman) who should be independent non-executive directors is:

A   Between 10% and 24%

B   Between 25% and 39%

C   Between 40% and 49%

D   50% or over

LO 5c, 5e

22 Fox plc's external (statutory) auditors have just won a contract with Fox plc to provide consultancy services.

Which of the following entities would usually be expected to examine the implications of this situation?

A   The board of directors

B   The remuneration committee

C   The audit committee

D   The non-executive directors

LO 5c, 5e, 5f

23 The appointment of suitably qualified, independent auditors is the responsibility of a listed company's:

A   Shareholders

B   Audit committee

C   Board of directors

D   Finance director

LO 5c, 5e, 5f

24 Sumatra plc operates its own internal audit function, choosing not to make use of an external supplier for these services. In light of this policy, it is vital that arrangements are established within the company to ensure that there is no compromise of the:

A   Independence of the internal auditors

B   Integrity of information security systems

C   Stewardship of directors

D   Rigour of financial reporting processes

LO 5e, 5f

Business and Finance: Question Bank

Chapter 13: The economic environment of business and finance

1   Anu Gupta trades as Reproduction, a manufacturer of classic furniture and furnishings. Anu predicts that 'if people's incomes rise next year, then the demand for our furniture will increase.' The accuracy of Anu's prediction depends on whether the furniture and furnishings the company produces:

    A   Are normal goods

    B   Have few substitutes

    C   Have many complements

    D   Have few complements

    LO 6a

2   A market trader has noticed that when the price of cakes rises, consumers tend to buy more biscuits instead. The effect operating here is:

    A   The income effect

    B   The diminishing marginal utility effect

    C   The substitution effect

    D   The price elasticity of demand

    LO 6a

3   If potatoes are a Giffen good, then an increase in the price of potatoes will cause:

    A   An increase in demand for potatoes

    B   A decrease in demand for substitutes for potatoes

    C   A decrease in demand for potatoes

    D   An increase in demand for substitutes for potatoes

    LO 6a

4   Which of the following is an example of complementary goods?

    A   Milk and orange juice

    B   Pepsi and Coca-Cola

    C   French fries and tomato sauce

    D   Lamb and beef

    LO 6a

5   An increase in the price of Y, a complement of X in consumption, will:

   A   Increase the demand for Y and decrease the demand for X

   B   Decrease the demand for Y and increase the demand for Y

   C   Increase the demand for both Y and X

   D   Decrease the demand for both Y and X

LO 6a

6   A particular brand of cheese is classified as an inferior good. Identify whether the following statements are true or false.

   Demand for the cheese will rise as incomes rise.

   A   True

   B   False

   Demand for the cheese only exists because of the effects of advertising.

   C   True

   D   False

LO 6a

7   Redium is a normal good which has become increasingly unfashionable during the past year. What changes to supply, demand and market price should this change in tastes have created?

   A   No impact on the demand curve, but a fall in market price and a fall in quantity supplied

   B   A shift in the demand curve to the right, a fall in market price and a fall in quantity supplied

   C   A shift in the demand curve to the left, a fall in market price and a fall in quantity supplied

   D   No impact on the demand curve, no impact on the supply curve but a fall in market price

LO 6a

8   If the market for a particular product is a natural monopoly then production of the product must be associated with:

   A   High marginal costs

   B   Low marginal costs

   C   Economies of scope acting as a barrier to entry

   D   Low fixed costs

LO 6b

9   Which of the following is an example of government intervention to correct a market failure?

   A   An increase in corporation tax during an economic boom

   B   An increase in the rate of VAT on all goods and services

   C   The taxation of goods with negative externalities

   D   The taxation of Giffen goods

LO 6b

10 The cross elasticity of demand between the Terra product and the Nova product is zero. It can, therefore, be deduced that the two products are:

   A   Complements

   B   Substitutes

   C   Veblen goods

   D   Unrelated

LO 6a

11 The price of Yellands has fallen by 4% in the last quarter, whilst in the same period demand for Dellows, where there has been no price change, has risen by 6.5%. The cross elasticity of demand between the two products is:

   A   – 1.625

   B   – 0.62

   C   1.625

   D   0.62

LO 6a

12 The UK government has recently imposed a maximum price on Pratex which is set at a level lower than its equilibrium price. In future, therefore, it can be expected that there will be:

   A   Excess supply of the product

   B   Excess demand for the product

   C   No effect on supply but an increase in demand

   D   No effect on demand but a decrease in supply

LO 6a, 6b

13 An analyst with Lanes plc has constructed a supply curve for one of the company's major products, the Ledo. The curve is actually a vertical straight line. This indicates that supply of the Ledo is:

A   Perfectly inelastic

B   Of unitary elasticity

C   Perfectly elastic

D   One

LO 6a

14 The Tempo product has experienced a significant rise in factor costs during recent months. Against this background, it can be expected that there will be:

A   A contraction in demand and supply

B   An expansion in demand and supply

C   A contraction in demand and an expansion in supply

D   An expansion in demand and a contraction in supply

LO 6a

15 In the market for the Optica product competitors tend not to compete through price, instead devoting substantial sums of money to raising consumer awareness through advertising. There is some degree of differentiation between products, often achieved through branding. There are many buyers and sellers in the market for the product. It would appear, therefore, that the market for the Optica product is one characterised by:

A   Monopolistic competition

B   Oligopoly

C   Perfect competition

D   Monopoly

LO 6b

16 Which THREE of the following are associated with conditions of perfect competition?

A   Suppliers are price-makers

B   Suppliers earn 'normal' profits

C   Consumers lack influence over market price

D   Differentiated products

E   A single selling price

LO 6b

17 Gromet plc has recently been able to achieve significant external economies of scale. This indicates that the market for the company's only product has been:

    A   Static, so forcing the company to achieve economies of scale in production

    B   Growing, so enabling the economies of scale to be achieved

    C   Contracting, so enabling the company to cut costs in distribution

    D   Volatile, meaning that internal economies of scale were unattainable

LO 6b

18 A shopkeeper finds that if he sets the price of a particular product at £9.00 per unit he sells, on average, 150 units of the product per month. However, at a price of £10.00 per unit, he sells an average of 110 units per month. The price elasticity of demand for the product is

    A   – 0.42

    B   – 2.40

    C   – 0.27

    D   – 0.11

LO 6a

19 If the minimum price for a good is set by the government above the current free market equilibrium price, what will be the effect (if any) on demand for and supply of the good in the short term?

Demand for the good

    A   Fall

    B   Rise

    C   No effect

Supply of the good

    D   Fall

    E   Rise

    F   No effect

LO 6a, 6b

20 Bench Ltd produces chairs. An economist working for the firm predicts that if average incomes rise next year, then demand for the firm's chairs will increase in direct proportion to the rise in incomes (assuming all other factors remain unchanged). The accuracy of the economist's prediction depends on whether the chairs produced by Bench Ltd:

    A   Are normal goods

    B   Have many complementary goods

    C   Have few complementary goods

    D   Have few substitutes

LO 6a

21   The basic economic problem facing all economies is:

A   Maximising economic growth

B   Unemployment

C   Inflation

D   Allocating scarce resources

LO 6c

22   Which of the following would NOT be regarded by economists as a factor of production?

A   Labour

B   Enterprise

C   Management

D   Capital

LO 6c

23   There are four main factors of production, each of which has an economic reward. Which one of the following statements about the factors of production is NOT correct?

A   Capital is rewarded with interest

B   Enterprise is rewarded with profit

C   Labour is rewarded with wages

D   Land is rewarded with property

LO 6c

24   Which of the following is NOT a source of economies of scale?

A   The introduction of specialist high-speed capital equipment

B   Bulk buying

C   The employment of specialist managers

D   Cost savings resulting from new production techniques

LO 3a

25   The marginal propensity to consume measures:

A   The relationship between changes in consumption and changes in consumer utility

B   The proportion of household incomes spent on consumer goods

C   The proportion of total national income spent on consumer goods

D   The relationship between changes in income and changes in consumption

LO 6c

26   Which of the following is the correct sequence in a business cycle?

A   Boom, Recession, Depression, Recovery

B   Recession, Recovery, Boom, Depression

C   Boom, Recovery, Recession, Depression

D   Recovery, Recession, Depression, Boom

LO 6c

27   The recession phase of the business cycle will normally be accompanied by all of the following EXCEPT which ONE?

A   A rise in the rate of inflation

B   A fall in the level of national output

C   An improvement in the trade balance

D   A rise in the level of unemployment

LO 6c

28   The government may seek to reduce the rate of demand-pull inflation by any of the following means EXCEPT:

A   Reducing interest rates

B   Increasing value added tax

C   Applying more stringent controls over bank lending

D   Reducing public expenditure

LO 6c

29   Which of the following would NOT lead to cost push inflation?

A   Rising import prices

B   Increase in wages

C   Increases in indirect taxation

D   High consumer expenditure such that aggregate demand exceeds aggregate supply

LO 6c

30 Which of the following are effects of reduced interest rates?

    (i)   Consumer spending will increase

    (ii) Business investment will be encouraged

    (iii) Saving will increase

    A   (i) only

    B   (i) and (ii)

    C   (ii) and (iii)

    D   All of them

LO 6c

31 Which of the following is an aspect of fiscal policy measures by the government?

    A   To raise short-term interest rates in the money markets

    B   To support the exchange rate for the country's currency

    C   To control growth in the money supply

    D   To alter rates of taxation

LO 6c

32 'Supply side' economics concerns:

    A   The behaviour of the microeconomic supply curve

    B   The supply of factors of production in response to changing levels of factor rewards

    C   The behaviour of the aggregate supply curve in connection with the levels of prices, incomes and employment

    D   The effect that an increase in the supply of money has on inflation

LO 6c

33 If the government wishes to increase consumer spending, it could increase the rate of:

    A   Income tax

    B   Corporation tax

    C   Import duties

    D   Social security payments

LO 6c

1   Intervention by the government to impose a limit on businesses' carbon emissions is an example of regulation motivated by the wish to address market failure caused by:

   A   Asymmetric information

   B   Equity

   C   Market imperfection

   D   Externalities

   LO 6b, 6d

---

2   The government recently passed regulations affecting the way in which car hire companies must address certain health and safety issues within their business. Speedy Hire plc is a major player in the UK car hire business. In anticipation of these new regulations the company actually put in place procedures and technology which exceed these new government regulations. From this it is clear that Speedy Hire plc's response to the new regulations has been one of:

   A   Innovation

   B   Entrenchment

   C   Mere compliance

   D   Full compliance

   LO 6d

---

3   Ferndale plc is a multinational company. It has recently been charged with being in breach of the Competition Act 1998 in respect of collusive behaviour in its UK operations. If found guilty, the company could, amongst other sanctions, face a fine of:

   A   Up to 10% of annual global revenues

   B   Up to 10% of annual UK revenues

   C   Up to 20% of annual global revenues

   D   Up to 20% of annual UK revenues

   LO 6d

---

4   The government is considering placing an additional tax on cigarettes to raise revenue to finance healthcare benefits. The demand for cigarettes is price inelastic. Which of the following statements is true?

    A   The tax on cigarettes may not raise as much revenue as anticipated in the years to come because the demand for cigarettes is likely to become more elastic over time

    B   This tax will not raise much revenue either in the short term or the long term since demand is price inelastic

    C   No tax revenue can be raised in this way because sellers of cigarettes will just lower their price by the amount of the tax and, therefore, the price of cigarettes to consumers will not change

    D   This is a very good way to raise revenue, both in the short term and in the long term, because there are no substitutes for cigarettes

LO 6d

5   Germand plc has been charged under the Competition Act 1998 with entering into an illegal anti-competitive agreement with one of its closest competitors. The company will clearly be charged with breaching:

    A   Chapter 1 of the Competition Act 1998

    B   Chapter 2 of the Competition Act 1998

    C   Chapter 3 of the Competition Act 1998

    D   Chapter 4 of the Competition Act 1998

LO 6d

6   Government intervention in a market economy can lead to an increase in economic welfare if:

    A   It sets a good's maximum price above its equilibrium price

    B   The market mechanism has failed to allow for externalities

    C   It sets a good's minimum price above its equilibrium price

    D   The demand for inferior goods rises as incomes increase

LO 6b, 6d

7   Which TWO of the following can refer cases for consideration to the Competition Commission?

    A   Government ministers

    B   Certain industry regulators

    C   Self-referral by the Commission

    D   A FTSE 100 company

    E   The London Stock Exchange

LO 6d

8   The Fenno product is manufactured in the UK but is also imported into the UK from France. The UK government has recently decided to apply an import quota on imports of the product from France at a level below the current level of imports. This action will have the effect of:

A   Only French suppliers suffering a lower price

B   Both UK and French suppliers suffering a lower price

C   Only UK suppliers enjoying a higher price

D   Both UK and French suppliers enjoying a higher price

LO 6f

9   Anti-monopoly legislation is an example of government intervention to address market failure caused by:

A   Market imperfection

B   Externality

C   Asymmetric information

D   Inequity

LO 6b, 6d

10 The Competition Act 1998 prohibits agreements, business practices and conduct that damage competition, including abuse of a dominant position. Examples of specific types of conduct that are particularly likely to be considered as an abuse where the business is in a dominant position include which THREE of the following?

A   Imposing transfer pricing

B   Limiting production markets or technical developments to the prejudice of consumers

C   Applying different trading conditions to equivalent transactions, thereby placing certain parties at a competitive disadvantage

D   Attaching unrelated supplementary conditions to contracts

E   Providing public goods on behalf of the government

LO 6b, 6d

11 In which of the following circumstances would a cartel be most likely to operate?

A   A market with a undifferentiated product and a large number of producers

B   A market with differentiated products and few producers

C   A market with a large number of producers and where demand for the product is inelastic

D   A market with few producers and an undifferentiated product

LO 6b, 6d

12 Supporters of anti-monopoly enforcement argue that the real gain from such enforcement is:

A   That it encourages firms to engage in research, which leads to new products being produced

B   That it serves to deter firms from engaging in such practices as collusion, price-fixing and deceptive advertising

C   That it forces firms to produce efficiently

D   The revenue generated from the fines paid by those individuals who are found guilty of anti-monopoly violations which can be used for socially worthwhile causes

LO 6b, 6d

13 Anti-monopoly laws are based on the proposition that the best way to achieve efficiency and the avoidance of excessive prices is through:

A   Regulation

B   Increased competition

C   Public ownership

D   Oligopoly

LO 6b, 6d

14 Identify whether each of the following statements regarding anti-monopoly legislation and market regulation are true or false.

Anti-monopoly legislation is undertaken to compensate for lack of competition, and market regulation is undertaken to promote competition

A   True

B   False

Anti-monopoly legislation is undertaken to promote competition and market regulation is undertaken to compensate for lack of competition

C   True

D   False

Anti-monopoly legislation is undertaken to promote competition and market regulation is also undertaken to promote competition

E   True

F   False

LO 6b, 6d

15 Any measures taken by government to redistribute wealth are a form of government intervention aimed at addressing problems concerned with:

A   Asymmetric information

B   Market imperfection

C   Lack of equity

D   Externalities

LO 6b, 6d

16 It is reported that two large listed companies recently colluded with each other to fix the price of a product they both sell in the UK market. Collusion of this type is an example of market failure due to:

A   Inequality of resources

B   External costs

C   Market power

D   Resource immobility

LO 6b, 6d

17 Webcraft plc, which has a dominant position in its markets, has received notice that it is being investigated under Chapter 1 of the Competition Act 1998.

Which of the following activities colluded in by Webcraft plc may, individually, have given rise to such a notice?

Limiting production markets

A   Yes

B   No

Agreeing with another organisation to limit competition

C   Yes

D   No

Restricting technical developments

E   Yes

F   No

LO 6b, 6d

Answer Bank

Chapter 1: Introduction to business

1   B, C and E

    An organisation is a social arrangement that pursues collective goals, that controls its own performance and, in addition, that has a boundary separating it from its environment. The other options are all ways that enable an organisation to increase productivity.

2   D   Profit-oriented organisations should aim to maximise shareholder wealth. Non-profit-oriented organisations, such as charities, should aim to provide goods and/or services.

3   A   Satisficing is when managers are not maximising wealth for owners (which they should, in fact, be doing) but are merely making enough profits to keep owners satisfied. Beyond that they often simply choose to pursue managerial objectives. This is the classic agency problem caused by the separation of ownership and control.

4   A,D,E

    Listed under the broad heading of product development, Joe might choose to bring in new products; develop a product range; invest in research and development; and/or provide products of a certain quality at a certain price level. If he were concentrating on employees and management to support his primary objective then he might aim to reduce labour turnover.

5   C   To double the share price within the next 10 years is most likely to be the primary business objective. The other three options would be typical secondary objectives for Avernanche plc in pursuit of the primary objective.

6   B   Baumol argued that businesses act to maximise sales revenue whenever managers are rewarded or revered for the size of the organisation for which they work rather than its profitability or relative performance.

7   A   Organisations whose primary objective is to make profits for their owners are classified as businesses.

8   A, B and E

    S = specific; M = measurable; A = achievable; R = relevant; T = time-bound

    The secondary objective is specific: market share is a manageable feature of the organisation; measurable: 20% is a quantifiable yardstick of attainment; time-bound: the deadline to complete the objective is within three years. There is no indication of factors that might indicate whether the secondary objective is either achievable or relevant.

9   A, B   The mission statement and vision are general expressions of the business's basic function and planned future status respectively, whilst shareholder wealth maximisation would rank as the primary objective of any organisation classified as a business.

10   B, C and D

    A mission statement should answer the following fundamental questions: What is our business? What is our value to the customer? What do we want our business to become? What should our business be? (A) and (F) are numerical targets and more likely to be secondary objectives; (E) is a detailed tactic.

11   A and C

The two groups most likely to put the company under pressure to improve its return on investment are the shareholders and the bankers. Customers want products of a certain quality at a reasonable price; suppliers are interested in regular orders in return for reliable delivery and good service; and employees' objectives include job security, good conditions of work and job satisfaction.

12   A   The primary objective (C) is the provision of medical services, whilst doing this efficiently would be an example of a secondary objective (D). Vision (A) concerns how the charity sees itself at some future time, whilst mission (B) is its basic function.

13   D   Trade unions are the stakeholders most likely to press for employee representation in the company's affairs.

14   A   The primary business objective of a profit-seeking plc will be the maximisation of shareholder wealth (A). The other statements are secondary objectives that will be pursued in support of this primary objective.

SAMPLE PAPER

15   B   This is the definition of sustainability as set out in the Brundtland report.

1   B   Referent power (B) is individual power based on identification with, admiration of or respect for the individual. This can be summed up as power based on force of personality. Legitimate power (A) is based on agreement and commonly held values which allow one person to have power over another person. It normally arises from position and derives from our cultural system of rights, obligations and duties in which a 'position' is accepted by people as being legitimate. Coercive power (C) enables a person to mediate punishments for others: for example, to dismiss, suspend, reprimand them, or make them carry out unpleasant tasks. Expert power (D) is based upon one person perceiving that the other person has expert knowledge of a given subject (often based on possession of formal qualifications) and is a recognised authority in a given situation.

2   C   The company's procedures allow the manager to authorise lendings up to £1m. This is legitimate power (C) – power given by his position and bank procedures. Referent power (A) – sometimes called personal power – is capable of influencing the behaviour of others. Trust, respect, charm and enthusiasm are all attributes that allow us to influence people without apparently imposing on them. Expert power (B) is the power that belongs to an individual because of his/her expertise. Reward power is power to grant promotion or pay increases (D).

3   B   Authority is the exercise of power for the proper purpose. Booking the business class seat is not within Cerise's authority, but she has had the power to persuade Malcolm nevertheless to book the seat. Delegation of authority (C) occurs where a superior gives to a subordinate the discretion to make decisions within a certain sphere of influence.

4   A   Accountability cannot be delegated so (B) and (D) are incorrect. Some power must be transferred by delegation if the person is to be able to accomplish the task for which they have been given authority and responsibility.

        Delegation embraces both authority and responsibility. Authority can be delegated readily, but many problems of delegation stem from failure to provide the necessary information and resources in order to achieve expected results, or from failure to delegate sufficient power for subordinates to fulfil their responsibilities.

5   A   Line authority refers to the relationship that exists between a manager and his/her direct staff, and occurs in most organisations. This line runs in an uninterrupted series of steps and is based on the scalar chain principle of hierarchy in which there is a clear line of authority from the top of the organisation to the bottom. Essentially, the scalar chain is used to implement decision-making and the issue of instructions.

6   B   A functional relationship means that a manager has authority in certain areas over another department. The IT manager could have functional authority over all other departments when defining rules for internet and email use. (C) is a line manager; (D) is a project manager; and (A) is a staff manager.

7   A   Mintzberg's managerial roles are interpersonal, informational and decisional. This is a simple Decision (A) for Andrew. The disseminator role (C) would form part of the informational role (D) and involves distributing information to staff, either as fact or as information involving some interpretation and integration. The interpersonal role (B) relates to such matters as listening to employee or giving feedback.

8   B   Charles is describing his interpersonal role (B) as a manager – representing his team in his capacity as their leader as well as interacting with managers of other teams within the company.

9   B   The forming stage (A) is associated primarily with seeking to define the purpose of the group (achieved at last week's meeting), but the storming stage (B) is where conflict first arises, particularly concerning competition for chosen roles. Once such conflicts have been addressed, the group will norm (C) and then, hopefully, perform (D).

10 B According to Quinn, when an organisational culture is outward-looking and high on control, it is termed a 'rational goal' culture (B). An internal process culture (A) is one in which the business looks inwards, aiming to make its internal environment stable and controlled. Goals are known and unchanging, and there are defined methods, rules and procedures governing all activities. Security, stability and order motivate staff. In an open systems culture (C) the external environment is a source of energy and opportunity, but it is ever-changing and unpredictable. The business must be highly flexible and open to new ideas, so is very adaptable in structure. Staff are motivated by growth, creativity and variety. In a human relations culture (D) the business looks inwards, aiming to maintain its existence and the well-being of staff. Staff are motivated by a sense of belonging.

11 A The marketing mix comprises four variables (A): product, price, promotion and place. The marketing mix is not the same as the sales mix (B) nor is it the same as the communications mix (D). It is also a broader concept than mere product features and benefits (C).

12 B The marketing orientation looks outwards and is concerned with ascertaining and supplying customers' requirements. Marketing is about supplying what the customer wants (B). The other statements show features of sales-orientation and product-orientation – a concentration on selling rather than marketing and a concentration on what we as a company have to offer (C) rather than on what the customer wants or needs. Instead of finding out what the customer wants, such a company would be trying to sell whatever items it happens to have in stock (A) or whatever Pemble staff thought innovative (D). Instead of a product-centred 'make and sell' philosophy, the marketing approach is a customer-centred 'sense and respond' philosophy.

13 C A staff function is one in which authority arises in giving specialist advice to another manager or department over which you have no line authority (C) and, therefore, no authority to make or influence decisions in that other department.

14 B, C and E

Attitudes, underlying competencies and skills, as well as communication patterns, are all classified as covert variables in the model. Formal goals (A) and organisation design (D) are overt variables.

15 B Market segmentation means that the market can be broken down into several sections (B) using segmentation bases such as age and gender. You can practise market segmentation and then target all the segments of the market (A) with a broad competitive scope (D). Markets are segmented into homogenous (ie distinct) groups of customers, each of them likely to react differently to a particular marketing mix. The fact that there are homogeneous sections within the total market, implies that the total market is heterogeneous rather than homogenous (C).

16 B,C,F

A general understanding of the marketing philosophy is absolutely essential for any business manager. If all staff are customer-oriented, then it is quite possible to practise marketing without a formal marketing department (F). Within a truly marketing-oriented organisation, everyone has a role to play and a contribution to make to the organisation's marketing success (C). The principal function of a company (B) is a reference to its mission, which is a much broader concept than marketing.

17 A TV advertising is addressed to consumers to 'pull' them in and encourage them to demand the goods (A). A push promotion (B) involves convincing trade intermediary channel members to 'push' the product through the distribution channels to the ultimate consumer via promotions and personal selling efforts. The company promotes the product through a reseller who in turn promotes it to yet another reseller or the final consumer. Trade promotion objectives are to persuade retailers or wholesalers to carry a brand, give a brand shelf space, promote a brand in advertising, and/or push a brand to final consumers. Car dealers often provide a good example of a combination of pull and push promotions (C). If you pay attention to car dealers' advertising, you will often hear them speak of cash-back offers and dealer incentives. Personal selling (D) involves the use of a sales force to support a push strategy (encouraging intermediaries to buy the product) or a pull strategy (where the role of the sales force may be limited to supporting retailers and providing after-sales service).

18　B　Status and ego needs (B) can be met by giving praise and promotion. Self-actualisation needs (A) are the individual's needs for realising his or her own potential, for continued self-development and creativity in its broadest sense. It is the need for a feeling of accomplishment and of being satisfied with oneself. Social needs (C) are the need to be part of a group. Safety (or security) needs (D) refer to the need for protection in all its senses.

19　A,C,F

As well as thinking that individuals dislike work and avoid it where possible, Statements 1 and 2 are assumptions of a manager who adopts a Theory X style of management, whilst Statement 3 is an assumption of a manager who adopts a Theory Y style of management. Other assumptions of the Theory Y style of management include the belief that, for most people, work is as natural as play or rest, the average worker can learn to accept and seek responsibility and people will exercise self-direction and self-control in the service of objectives to which they are committed.

20　A,C,F

Working conditions and relations with the boss are both hygiene factors. Challenging work is a motivating factor.

21　D　Dividing a market into homogeneous groups of potential customers who may be treated similarly for marketing purposes is the process of market segmentation (D). The marketing mix comprises the 4 or the 7 Ps, while the marketing orientation describes the focus of the firm as a whole. Market research is the process of finding out more about a particular market or market segment.

22　A　A business which accepts the needs of potential customers as the basis for its operations, and whose success is seen as being dependent on developing and marketing products that satisfy those needs would be described as having a marketing orientation (A). A sales orientation (B) is found in businesses that see their main purpose as being just to sell more of the products or services which they already have available. A product orientation (C) usually means that the business focuses on the product and its features and effectively forgets what it is that the customer needs and wants, while a business with a production orientation (D) is just preoccupied with making as many units as possible; customer needs are subordinated to the desire to increase output.

23　C　The main influences are costs, competitors, customers and corporate objectives (C). The concepts in A and D are those of the marketing mix, while those in B relate to operations management.

24　B　High volume lends itself to Harris plc's capital-intensive operation, with specialisation of work and well-established systems for getting the work done. Unit costs should therefore be low (B).

25　C　Research into products which have obvious commercial or practical use is called applied research (C). Market research (A) is into the market itself, not the product, while process research (D) is into processes rather than products. The aim of pure research (B) is to obtain new scientific or technical knowledge or understanding. There is no obvious commercial or practical end in view.

26　B　The four elements of the procurement mix are quantity, quality, price and lead time (B). Price, product, place and promotion (A) are the four elements of the product marketing mix, while volume, variety, variation in demand and visibility (C) are the four Vs of operations management. Costs, competitors, customers and corporate objectives (D) are the four Cs of pricing.

1   B,C,E

The degree of decentralisation is a measure of how power and authority are passed down an organisation. This is not shown on an organisation chart, which concentrates on the shape of the organisation. The span of control refers to the number of subordinates working for a superior, while the scalar chain is the formal arrangement of authority or the organisation hierarchy. Both are shown on the chart.

2   C   A professional bureaucracy (C) will hire trained specialists who are all imbued with the skills and values of the profession. The operating core is the key part because it will have an elaborate support staff to service it and the work is too complex to be standardised by a technostructure. The entrepreneurial structure (A) is characteristic of small, young organisations revolving round a single entrepreneur or small management team. A machine bureaucracy (B) works on a sophisticated and well-tuned set of rules and procedures. The technostructure is the key part of this structure and the management philosophy is often that of scientific management. There is strong emphasis on the division of labour and authority is hierarchical. A divisional structure (D) is where the middle line seeks as much autonomy for itself as possible. It exerts a pull to split into small self-managed units with autonomy given to managers lower down the line.

3   A,B,E

The support staff (A) carry out the ancillary activities that are neither part of the core nor the technostructure. Support staff have no role in the direct activities of the organisation: these activities include such things as catering and public relations. The middle line (B) represents that part of the organisation where the middle managers operate. Its role is to turn the instructions of the strategic apex into activities for the operating core. The ideology (E) is what binds the organisation together. It represents the organisational values and beliefs, which provide a common focus for all the other elements.

Functional division (C) and matrix (F) structures are both types of organisational structure, and scalar chain (D) is the reporting chain.

4   C   The function of the technostructure is to standardise work processes (C), for example by producing technical specifications and procedures manuals. The strategic apex, which represents the higher management of the organisation, will ensure the organisation follows its mission (A). The support staff provide ancillary services (B) to the operating core. The middle line, representing the managers between the operating core and the strategic apex, will control the work of the operating core (D).

5   A   Machine bureaucracy depends primarily on the standardisation of its operating work processes (A) for co-ordination. Because of that the technostructure, which houses the analysts (technocrats) who do the standardising, emerges as the key part of the structure. When the operating core exerts a pull towards standardised skills (B), it is generally a professional bureaucracy. In a divisionalised structure, a good deal of power is delegated to market-based units in the middle line (C), whose efforts are coordinated by the standardisation of outputs through the extensive use of performance control systems. Adhocracy coordinates primarily by mutual adjustment among all of its parts, calling especially for the collaboration of its support staff (D).

6   A   Unity of command (A) means that any employee should have to report to, or receive orders from, only one manager. 'Unity of direction' is the principle that there should be only one manager of each activity (B). 'Scalar chain' is the term used to describe the chain of superiors from the lowest to the highest rank (C). 'Division of work' is the principle of specialisation of work into particular tasks (D).

7   C   A matrix structure would involve employees within the project team having responsibility to more than one superior – for example, a functional supervisor and a project leader. This breaks the principle of unity of command (C), which holds that any employee should have to report to, or receive orders from, only one boss. There is no reason why a matrix structure should contravene the principle of authority and responsibility (A) as employees can be given both in such a structure. Similarly, subordination of individual interests (B) – the principle that the interest of one or more employees should not prevail over that of the general interest of the organisation – would apply to a matrix structure, like any other. Esprit de corps (D) is the principle that personnel should not be isolated (cohesion should be encouraged), which would be ideal in this matrix setting.

8   B,C,E

Decentralisation depends on workforce ability (B), company size (C) – the larger the organisation, the harder it is to centralise – and effective communication (E), which is an essential ingredient of effective delegation. Centralisation and decentralisation refer to the extent to which authority for decision-making is either retained at the top of the organisation or delegated to lower levels.

If the management style is authoritarian (A), the organisation will be more centralised.

Slow technological change (D) means that there is little need to decentralise. Lower level managers do not need to be familiar with changing technology.

9   A   If employees are all carrying out the same or similar tasks (A), a supervisor will be more able to look after many subordinates (a wider span of control) as they can all be handled in similar ways and will face similar problems. A high geographical dispersion of employees (B) requires more effort to supervise which, along with frequent time-consuming problems (C), suggests a narrow span of control would be more appropriate. Where the manager is engaged in large amounts of non-supervisory work (D), the narrower the span of control is likely to be.

10   A,D,E

A wide, flat organisation implies looking after many subordinates, so delegation will be called upon frequently (A). The vertical flow of information between the top and bottom of the company follows a shorter, more efficient route in a wide, flat organisation (D), so communication is likely to be improved. Looking after many employees implies large spans of control (E).

The features you would expect to see in a tall narrow organisation are higher administration and overhead costs (B) to support the many levels within the structure; many opportunities for promotion (C) because there are more rungs in the ladder to the top; and slow decision-making (F) because the management structure requires more co-ordination and consultation before decisions are taken.

11   A   If there are many subordinates to supervise, as there would be in a wide, flat organisation, it can be difficult to give each enough individual time (A). High management overhead costs (B), internal communication difficulties (C) and superiors not delegating enough work to staff (D) are problems associated with tall, narrow organisational structures.

12   A,B,F

If a shareholder dies, their shares are transferred to another person without any effect on the company at all – this is known as 'perpetual succession' (A). A limited company is legally distinct from its owners – it has a separate legal identity (B). Limited companies, both private and public, are subject to stringent regulations governing the keeping of accounting records, the filing of financial statements and the annual return with the Registrar and in the case of larger companies, the requirement to have an audit (F). Withdrawal of capital (D) is relatively difficult as it provides a buffer for creditors. A limited company's liability is unlimited (E) – it is the liability of the owners (shareholders) that is limited. Because financial statements are filed they are not private (C).

13 D,H Mechanistic organisations are machine-like and efficient at performing the same task over and over, implying a slow-moving environment (D). Organic organisations are flexible and adaptable (like a living organism), implying they are suitable for dynamic environments (D). Employees working for a mechanistic organisation are expected to obey superiors, whereas for those working for an organic organisation, commitment to mission is more highly valued than loyalty as such. In terms of structure of control, the network structure is more prevalent in organic organisations as is the relatively flexible job descriptions. Precise job descriptions and hierarchical structure of control are typical features of a mechanistic organisation.

14 A,C,F

The company could be described as a bureaucracy or mechanistic organisation. As well as innovation being suppressed (statement 1), this type of structure can inhibit creativity, initiative and openness to new ideas and ways of doing things. People would certainly be concerned with completing the task efficiently (statement 2) – task specification and efficiency is a feature of a bureaucratic design. Jobs are generally broken down into narrow areas of work/responsibility so as to secure the benefits of specialisation. In bureaucracies it is hard to learn from mistakes (statement 3) due to the lack of feedback (especially upwards).

15 B,C,E

In times of change, the Theory Y manager (B) recognises that the employees' objectives will complement those of the organisation and commitment is a function of the 'intrinsic' rewards associated with their achievement (rather than just extrinsic rewards/punishments). The capacity to exercise imagination, ingenuity and creativity in the solution of organisational problems needs to be widely rather than narrowly distributed in the workforce. Wide, flat organisations (C) tend to be flexible and employees are willing to form teams to tackle issues. Wide, flat organisations also imply a large amount of delegation (E) is needed.

16 C,D Group structure implies one company owning one or more subsidiaries. Joint venture implies that a third party business is set up and owned by the joint venturers. A strategic alliance is fairly informal co-operation. In this circumstance, there is no new separate legal company, as would be expected for a joint venture.

17 C   Only the limited liability partnership (C) necessarily exists as an entity separate from its owners. A general partnership (B) is not a separate legal entity from the partners. A joint venture between two limited liability companies (A) is usually a limited company but does not necessarily have to be established in that way. A strategic alliance (D) is an informal contractual or minority cross shareholding arrangement. Normally no separate company is formed.

18 A,B A floating charge (which gives lenders security for their loan) cannot be created over the business of a sole trader (A), but it can be over the assets of a limited company. This could hinder her ability to raise finance. Currently, Angela has unlimited liability (B) and with the increasing financial commitments of the business it might be better for her personally to seek limited liability, though the business will still have unlimited liability for its own debts (C). As a sole trader, the business's liability is not distinct from her own. Filing financial statements at Companies House (D), and the rules that apply to the business's constitution (E), do not apply to Angela as she is not operating as a company.

19 B   Partners' capital represents partners' stakes, or ownership, of a business. So do shares. In the absence of cash changing hands, the shares must therefore match the partners' capital amounts (B), which are unlikely to be in the profit-sharing ratio 3:2:1. A business which trades as a company may be no different from a partnership in any other way than in one important fact: while partners as owners take all the risks in the business having (generally) unlimited liability for the debts of the business, the owners of a company (its shareholders) have limited liability for its debts beyond any amount they may still owe for the shares they hold. The creditors of the business will be in the same position after incorporation (C). Dividends will be paid according to shares held (D).

20   C   A strategic alliance (C) is an informal or weak contractual agreement between companies. A licensing agreement (A) would be more formal in nature (based on a legally binding contract to ensure adherence to agreements), whilst a joint venture (B) would nearly always involve the formation of a separate company, with the investing companies taking a financial stake as shareholders and with management being provided as agreed. A group structure (D) would imply the establishment of a new company that would be controlled by one of the two companies.

21   B,D,E

Sales management – No

Financial reporting for the London Stock Exchange – No

Periodic management accounts – Yes

Sales management is part of both marketing and operations, so would be handled by Rumbert Insurance itself, not by the Regional Office. Financial reporting is centralised at Head Office so again would not be provided by the Regional Office. Periodic management accounts would be provided by the Regional Office as they are neither marketing/operations, nor are they related to strategic direction or consolidated financial reporting.   SAMPLE PAPER

22   B,C,E

A strategic alliance – No separate legal identity

A limited liability partnership – Separate legal identity

A registered company – Separate legal identity

A strategic alliance is an informal or weak contractual agreement between parties or a minority cross-shareholding arrangement, neither of which imply a separate legal identity from the owners. Both companies and limited liability partnerships are separate legal entities.   SAMPLE PAPER

23   B,C,F

It prevents him from employing staff	False
It gives him personal liability for any failure	True
It prevents him from obtaining a loan	False

As a sole trader he can raise loans and employ staff so neither of these statements is true. However, as a sole trader he does have the disadvantage of personal liability.   SAMPLE PAPER

24   B   Shareholders do not have an automatic right to be a director or to be involved in management (C). The partners' individual shareholdings will be determined by an agreement that is not necessarily related to the existing partnership agreement (A). The concept of perpetual succession means that the company will not dissolve upon the death of a shareholder (D).   SAMPLE PAPER

25   A,F,H

Buy Secateur Ltd – Group structure

Form a project team – Strategic alliance

With Secateur Ltd as equal partner – Joint venture

Purchasing the company will make it part of a group; forming a project team is a form of strategic alliance. Plicateur Ltd would be a separate legal entity owned 50:50 by the two companies and this is the most usual form of joint venture. A strategic alliance is more informal.   SAMPLE PAPER

1   A   Home computers would be referred to as either (C) and (D) since those two terms can be used interchangeably. A particular manufacturer's brand version of a home computer would be (B). Laptop or desktop computers would both be examples of product form (A).

2   A, C and E

Options (B) and (D) are methods of analysing the company's external environment – B analyses the task (or market) environment, whilst D analyses the macroenvironment. (F) is a means of assessing potential growth strategies of the company.

3   B   Age is a demographic factor that falls under the Social aspect of PESTEL analysis (B). P = political, T = technological, L = legal.

4   C   A functional strategy (A) would be concerned with the role of the marketing function itself within the company. Competitive strategy (C) is concerned with how the business will compete in terms of source of competitive advantage (cost or differentiation) and extent of competitive scope (broad or narrow). Product/market strategy (D) is concerned with how the business will grow (Ansoff's Matrix). Business strategy (B) is concerned in particular with how the marketing mix would be adjusted in due course if a competitive strategy of differentiation was decided upon.

5   A and B

High initial capital costs (A) add risk to a project by increasing the break-even point and necessitating that a large customer base is built up relatively quickly. This can deter new entrants. The relatively concentrated customer base (B) means that existing players have a distinct advantage and it also gives the customers higher bargaining power and makes the sector less attractive to new entrants. C may increase rivalry but it does not affect new entrants; (D) has no effect.

6   D   Low levels of competition in an industry make it more attractive for new entrants. High capital costs involve risk and fund raising challenges which can act as a barrier to new entrants.

7   D   In terms of Mendelow's matrix, this stakeholder clearly possesses both a high level of interest in the company's affairs and a high level of power (influence) over them. In such circumstances, the recommended strategy is one of treating the stakeholder concerned as a key player.

8   D   The exclusivity of the holidays indicates an emphasis on generating competitive advantage through differentiation rather than low cost, whilst their specialist nature and precise target market (age 60+) indicate a focus strategy rather than a broad competitive scope.

9   C   With a low market share of a high growth market, the Pluton would be classified as a Question mark within the BCG matrix, for which the possible recommended strategies are Build or Harvest. Option (A) relates to a Dog, option (B) to a Cash Cow and option (D) to a Star.

10 C   The company is introducing a new product but clearly targeted at the same market as its existing products, hence growth by means of product development.

11 B, C and D

Johnson and Scholes recommend evaluating strategies against the following criteria:

Suitability – does the strategy fit the strengths, objectives and image of the company?

Feasibility – does the company have the necessary resources to pursue the strategy effectively?

Acceptability – is the strategy acceptable to the company's stakeholders?

12   B   With a high market share in a low/no growth market, the Zulon is clearly a Cash Cow. The two strategy options are Hold (which implies continuing to support the product financially to maintain its position) or Harvest (which implies running down investment in the product and just managing the product for cash flow during its final years). The product manager appears to rule out the Hold strategy (withdraw investment), hence Harvest is the key (B).

13   C   The decline phase starts after the maturity phase ends, but the diagram will not predict when that will be (A). Sales growth is never guaranteed – the introduction could be a flop (B). There is a vast range of mature phase lengths and it cannot be said that they are usually 10 years (D). The maturity phase is the phase during which profits from the product are usually maximised (C).

14   B   In the positioning-based view of strategic planning (B) the competitive forces at work in the industry are the driving force behind strategy. In the resource-based view of strategic planning (C), the business's strategic capabilities are the driving force behind strategy. Charles appears to be adopting a formal rather than an emergent approach (A) and there is no evidence of gap analysis (D).

15   B   Millward Ltd is consistently aggressive in its responses to competitor actions – a 'tiger' reaction profile (B).

16   C, D and E

      Differentiation means distinguishing your products and services from competitors' offerings in ways that target customers will value. Therefore, better products using superior component parts (E), distinctive branding (D) and improved features and benefits (C) can all help. Options (A) and (B) would most likely underpin a competitive strategy based on low cost rather than differentiation.

17   C   The companies offer distinctly different products that satisfy different needs but which are highly likely to be competing for the same disposable income. They are, therefore, generic competitors (C).

18   A, D and E

      (B) and (C) are both support activities in the value chain model.

19   B,F

      A plan setting out the markets – Business plan

      A plan setting out how overall objectives will be achieved – Operational plan

      An operational plan specifies what is expected of each function in a business and a business plan sets out the market(s) to be served, how they will be served and the finance required.
                                                          SAMPLE PAPER

20   C   Strengths and weaknesses (A) would be revealed by a SWOT analysis; the structure of an industry would be revealed by a Five Forces Analysis (B); and helping to identify the relative levels of interest and power (D) refers to stakeholder mapping. A PESTEL analysis (C) reveals the key influences in the organisation's macro-environment (rather than its market or task environment).   SAMPLE PAPER

21   A,D

Offering its distribution capability to other supermarkets	Corporate strategy
Training store staff in the handling of personal safety issues	Not a corporate strategy

      Training store staff is very much an operational issue that does not constitute a corporate strategy, but offering its capability to other supermarkets is a fundamental long-term 'directional' decision which commits the company's resources.   SAMPLE PAPER

22 A,C

Government subsidies removed	Indicates increased rivalry
Two key customers merge	Indicates increased rivalry

A concentration of customers will increase rivalry since the power of customers is thereby increased. Removal of government subsidies creates a more level playing field amongst competitors hence increasing rivalry.   SAMPLE PAPER

23 A   Focusing on matching its internal strengths and weaknesses with its external opportunities and threats means that the business sees strategy as being about its position (A) in its environment and its market, according to Mintzberg.

24 C   With respect to an industry's life cycle, it is the maturity stage – which can last for a very long time – during which competition would be expected to be most intense (C). In the growth stage (B) there is still market enough for everyone, while in the introduction (A) and decline (D) stages there are far fewer participants in the industry.

Chapter 5: Introduction to risk management

1   A   (B) Is strategy risk, (C) Is product risk and (D) Is market risk.

2   C   Fixed costs have to be paid irrespective of the level of production or activity achieved. The higher the proportion of fixed costs the greater is the financial risk as, if business activity falls, it might not be possible to cover these costs.

3   D   Appetite for risk (D) is the extent to which you are willing to take on risk. Being risk averse means that you prefer to take the investment with the lowest risk.

4   C,E   Risk is the variation in an outcome while uncertainty denotes a lack of information.

5   A   Risk reduction (B) would imply taking action to prevent any chance of the product catching fire; risk acceptance (D) would imply doing nothing and proceeding to launch the product; risk transfer (C) might imply taking out liability insurance or selling the product on the basis of no liability in the event of fire. By not going ahead the company is simply avoiding the risk (A).

6   B,D   If there are two investments offering different risks, a risk seeking investor will always prefer the one with the higher risk. If there are two investments offering different returns, a risk neutral investor will always prefer the one with the higher return, regardless of the risk.

7   B   Gross risk is a function of the loss or impact and its probability, before any control measures are implemented.

8   C   This is clearly regulatory risk, which is a form of event risk.

9   B   All the outcomes and the probability of them occurring are known. As a result, there is no uncertainty, only risk.

10   D   A risk minimising investor will always choose the lowest risk investments, whatever their potential return.

11   C   Risk exposure is simply a measure of the way a business is faced by risks, whether financial, business, event etc.

12   B   First the company should see if the risk can be avoided; if not, it should try to reduce it; having reduced it as far as is feasible, it should explore the possibilities for sharing the risk (eg using insurance). Finally it must accept the remaining risk.

13   B   Where a risk falls into the low impact, high probability quadrant of the risk map the most appropriate response is risk reduction, focusing on reducing the likelihood of the adverse event occurring.

14   C   Management controls include all aspects of management that ensure the business is properly planned, controlled and led, including the organisation's structure.

15   C   Insurance transfers risk (C). In return for an insurance premium, the insurance company agrees to take on an agreed proportion of the financial burden of a risk.

16   A   These risks are to do with the operations of the business – a process going wrong, a valued employee leaving, a regulation being broken.

17   C   The nature of the imaging business has changed through new technology bringing innovations. The company's main business has radically fallen because of this: it has suffered product business risk.

18   A   Both changes (machinery and borrowing) increase the company's financial risk as they increase the amounts (fixed overheads and interest) that have to be paid irrespective of how much production is achieved. They both mean that the company is more exposed if there is a downturn in demand for its products.

19   D   The failure of a participant in the business's supply chain to honour their contractual obligations is classified as systemic risk which is a specific sub-section of event risk.

20   B   Following risk awareness and identification (3), the risk manager analyses and measures the risk (2) and assesses how it can be responded to and controlled (1). The risk is then monitored and reported (4).

21   B   Clearly the company is not retaining the risk by outsourcing (D). The risk still exists so it is not avoided (C), and outsourcing does not necessarily reduce the probability or impact. Instead, the risk is transferred (B).   SAMPLE PAPER

22   A,D,E

     Product risk – Business risk

     Event risk – Non-business risk

     Economic risk – Business risk

     Business risk arises from the nature of the business, its operations and the conditions it operates in; this includes product risk and economic risk. Non-business risk relates to all other types of risk, including principally financial risk and event risk.   SAMPLE PAPER

Chapter 6: Introduction to financial information

1   C   Tactical information (C) helps staff deal with short-term issues and opportunities. Operational information (B) is concerned with day-to-day issues. Strategic information (D) has longer-term concerns than both tactical and operational information. Planning information specifically helps staff involved in the planning process (A).

2   D   Systems sit within an environmental setting (D).

3   A   Structured decisions can be reduced to a series of rules which, if followed, will lead to the correct decision being made. This is what management information systems specialise in.

4   B,C   A range check can give some assurance that a value is accurate (for example, months in a date should be from 1 to 12). A range check can give no assurance that all transactions have been accounted for.

5   A,C   A pre-established control total will reconcile if data is subsequently entered inaccurately or not all data is entered. The control total, therefore, addresses both completeness and accuracy.

6   B   The manager's comments are simply a definition of the ACIANA quality of data integrity. It is achieved by preventing accidental or deliberate but unauthorised insertion, modification or destruction of data in the database.

7   A, B and C

The log should help to prevent (A) unauthorised processing as processing privileges are defined by the log-in details. Because any transaction can be traced to the perpetrator, the log will aid detection (B) and deterrence (C). The log can do little about correction, completeness or accuracy of what the user enters.

8   D   A management information system concentrates on producing useful reports from internal data. Much of the internal data will arise from transactions that have been recorded by the transaction processing system.

9   A and B

Strategic information is used by an organisation's senior management to plan its long-term future. Therefore, much use is made of estimates (A) about future sales, costs etc, and because strategic planning is undertaken at a level removed from day-to-operations the information is likely to be highly aggregated (B). Characteristics (C) and (D) are very much associated with operational information.

10   C, E and F

This is based on the ACCURATE model of good information. Information does not need to be detailed (A); in fact, too much detail could detract from it by undermining its ease of use. Nor does it have to be immediate (B) – it only needs to be available when it is required (timely). Profuse (D) implies lots of information and this can obscure the important information which could undermine both relevance and ease of use.

11   A, D   The data is both accurate and complete, so as data it must be classed as good data. However, the report is completely inappropriate for the sales director – too much detail, no aggregation, not particularly relevant – so it fails the ACCURATE requirements of being easy to use, user-targeted, relevant or cost-beneficial.

12   C, D and E

All external information will be missed or ignored by this closed system. Therefore, there will be no information about competitors, legislation or share price.

13   C   These terms are part of an expert system. The knowledge base contains the expert's set of decision-making rules and the inference engine applies the rules to the given circumstances.

14 B The major problem with the internet is uncertainty regarding whether the source is a reliable one, ie whether it is authoritative.

15 D Comparability from one year to the next is helped by companies choosing a particular accounting policy and remaining with it.

16 C In addition to helping users make decisions, the *Conceptual Framework for Financial Reporting* states that financial information, in general, is useful when it shows the results of management's stewardship of the resources entrusted to it, so that managers are thereby accountable to shareholders.

17 D When financial information influences the decisions of users then it is said to be relevant.

18 D Authorisation, in this context, is defined as the fact that changes can only be made by accountable individuals. It is one of the ACIANA qualities of a secure system.

19 C Non-repudiation refers to the fact that information should not be open to being rejected by its recipients on the grounds of faults in the information system. It is one of the ACIANA qualities of a secure system.

20 A,D,E

Its lack of timeliness – Undermines usefulness

The high level of regulation – Does not undermine usefulness

The high level of aggregation it contains – Undermines usefulness

By definition financial statements are produced some months after a company's financial year end so the information they contain is not timely; lack of timeliness undermines relevance, though figures may thereby be more reliable. The level of aggregation in the figures can obscure important details and so undermine usefulness. The level of regulation, however, adds to reliability and comparability both of which add to rather than detract from their usefulness. SAMPLE PAPER

21 A,D,E

Completeness – Key

Non-repudiation – Not key

Verifiability – Key

To be effective, information processing should meet the CATIVA criteria – completeness, accuracy, timeliness, inalterability, verifiability and assessability. Non-repudiation is one of the ACIANA qualities of information systems security. SAMPLE PAPER

22 B External users do not have access to management accounting information (A) and (C). Financial reporting does provide information to both managers and people outside the company, such as investors (B) but it is not confidential (D).

23 B,C These are the fundamental qualitative characteristics. The enhancing qualitative characteristics are understandability, comparability, verifiability and timeliness. If financial statements demonstrate at least the fundamental characteristics then investors will be able to rely on them in making their decisions; this reliance is enhanced if the further characteristics are also displayed.

24 D General purpose financial statements are used by investors, payables (creditors) and management.

25 D Good quality information must be accurate (A) and timely (C), and valuable information must be accessible (B), but to be both good quality and valuable it must be relevant (D).

26   B   An information system which combines data and analytical models or data analysis tools to help with semi-structured and unstructured problem solving and decision making in an operational context is a decision support system (B). An expert support system (A) is a sophisticated database that pools data from internal and external sources and makes information available to senior managers in an easy-to-use form so they can make strategic, unstructured decisions. A knowledge work system (C) facilitates the creation and integration of new knowledge into an organisation while an office automation system (D) increases the productivity of data and information workers.

Chapter 7: The business's finance function

1   B   Ensuring that resources are properly controlled or stewardship is part of the finance function's task of recording financial transactions.

2   B   The internal rate of return (B) is a capital budgeting technique that uses discounted cash flow principles. The internal rate of return of an investment project is the discount rate which, when applied to a project's net cash flows, results in a zero net present value.

3   D   Centralisation of the finance function generally works very well for transaction recording, external reporting and cash management, but it is often found to be less useful in terms of supporting the achievement of organisational objectives when it comes to internal reporting on performance to managers.

4   B   Net present value (B) takes the time value of money into account by discounting cash flows to their present value. Payback period (A) takes account of actual cash flows and not the time value of money. Return on investment (C) and return on capital (D) use figures straight from the financial statements and do not apply any discounting.

5   A,D,E

       Budgets might form the basis of a cash flow forecast (B) but not a statement of cash flows, which is a backward-looking document included in the financial statements. Whilst assisting in the co-ordination of activities is a commonly quoted purpose of budgets, this would not relate specifically to the co-ordination of financial reporting activities (C) as budgeting is a management accounting rather than a financial reporting activity.

6   C   Treasury management (C) is concerned with managing the funds of a business, namely cash and other working capital items plus long-term investments, short-term and long-term debt and equity finance.

7   A,E,F

       Management accounts are internal accounts used for managing the business. Financial reporting is regulated by accounting standards and statute (B) and report on historical results. Financial statements are used by shareholders (C). Therefore, management accounts can look forward and backwards (A), will probably have a cash flow forecast (E) – a statement of cash flows is an historical summary of cash flows and forms part of the financial statements – and will almost certainly have budgetary information (F) to assist planning.

8   D   Rolling budgeting means that as each month goes by the budgets for the months ahead are reviewed and, if necessary, revised so that they remain relevant for the remainder of the budget period.

9   A   Financial reporting involves preparing financial information including the financial statements, tax and regulatory reporting.

10   C   The Turnbull guidance refers to the need, amongst other things, to focus on the extent and categories of risk which the company regards as acceptable.

11   B   If the proportion of fixed costs increases, then profits are more susceptible to a fall in sales volume, as the fall in sales volume will not be accompanied by the same proportionate fall in costs than was previously the case when variable cost were a higher proportion of total costs.

12   C   Capital investment appraisal techniques such as net present value discount estimated future cash flows back to their present value so that the company has an absolute measure expressed to today's terms of the extent to which any investment is adding to or detracting from shareholder wealth.

13   A   Flexible budgeting involves adjusting the budget for a period to reflect actual levels of activity.

14 A   The time value of money is the value of a cash flow at an identified time in the future measured in terms of cash held now. It is therefore a key issue when appraising which projects should be invested in now to generate cash flows in the future (A). Capital budgeting (B) is concerned entirely with the here and now, in planning how limited capital available now should be spent. Pricing (C) is influenced by costs, competitors, customers and corporate objectives. Forecasting (D) considers what is going to happen and what the organisation can plan to do about it. It is an issue in capital investment appraisal but is not directly concerned with the time value of money.

15 C   Managers have stewardship over resources owned by the shareholders, so the shareholders (C) use the financial statements to assess the quality and effectiveness of their stewardship. Shareholders own shares (which are risky investments) in the hope of earning a satisfactory return. Community representatives (A), employees (B) and managers (D) have other primary interests.   SAMPLE PAPER

16 C   Record-keeping and stewardship (A) relates to double-entry bookkeeping; planning/control (B) is not a function of financial statements which essentially look back at past financial performance and position. Financial statements are not primarily aimed at an internal audience (D), which is the role of management accounting. External reporting is financial reporting (C) – producing financial statements which are used primarily by external users.
                                                                                SAMPLE PAPER

17 A   Management accounting is driven not by rules or standards but by the need to meet the information requirements of managers (A) within an organisation who use the information to plan, control, make decisions and monitor performance.   SAMPLE PAPER

18 D   The balanced scorecard is a performance measurement tool (D) focused on a variety of performance measures important to a business, rather than purely financial ones.
                                                                                SAMPLE PAPER

19 B,C,E

Financial management – No

Transactions recording – Yes

The role of non-executive directors – Yes

POB sets out that maintaining control and safeguarding assets involves: recording transactions; ensuring internal controls are sufficient; ensuring the audit committee is properly constituted and resourced; ensuring there are qualified and resourced non-executive directors.
                                                                                SAMPLE PAPER

20 A,C,D

Any control system should have these three major components. However, while identification of deviations from the plan (B) is part of the control process, where there are deviations from plan a decision has to be made as to whether to adjust the plan (eg it was not achievable) or the performance (eg it was sub-standard) so this stage is part of the follow up. Measuring an ideal level of performance (E) is useful but becomes valuable information only when it is used to identify the planned performance. Devising a plan (F) is where the whole exercise begins but any plan needs targets and standards to act as performance indicators.

21 B   Effectiveness is the measure of achievement and the extent to which objectives have been attained (3). Efficiency is the relationship between outputs and the resources used to produce those outputs. An efficient operation produces the maximum output for any given set of resource inputs (2); or it has minimum inputs for any given quantity and quality of output. Economy means obtaining the appropriate quantity and quality of inputs at the lowest cost (1). An activity would not be economic, if, for example, there was over-staffing or failure to purchase materials of requisite quality at the lowest available price.

22 D   High quality might be more important than costs, high margins might be more important than revenue. We cannot therefore state that either low costs or high sales revenue will always be CSFs.

23 D Economy is measured by the success of the team or work group in controlling its costs (D). The amount of resources used for the tasks that have been achieved (A) would be a measure of efficiency. Effectiveness would be measured by the organisation's performance in achieving its goals and targets (B). Team member satisfaction and the motivational climate cannot be used to measure economy (C).

24 A,F Liquidity is the main concern for suppliers.

Risk and return are the main concern of shareholders.

25 C,D,H

Effectiveness – Both

Economy – PTN

Productivity – Uist plc

Both organisations will want to be effective in doing what they do. A not-for-profit organisation such as a charity will want to be effective whilst operating in an economical fashion; a profit-making manufacturing organisation will want to ensure that its resources are used in the most productive fashion but not necessarily the cheapest.   SAMPLE PAPER

26 B The triple bottom line measures an organisation's performance in terms of its achievement of sustainability goals relating to social, economic and environmental factors.

1   C   Short-term funds are those used to cover normal operations and can be taken to mean finance available for up to one year. An example is debt factoring (C). Bank loans and mortgages are debt finance provided for more than one year, while share capital is equity finance that is also provided for more than one year.

2   A   All businesses face a trade-off between being profitable and being liquid. Less liquidity may yield greater profitability, but less liquidity equals greater risk (A). As both inventory and receivables (B) are current assets the trade-off between these does not affect the overall level of current assets. The equity and debt (C) trade-off is concerned with long-term capital structure rather than current assets and the short-term versus long-term borrowing trade-off (D) is a financing decision unrelated to current assets.

3   A   The transactions motive means that a business holds cash to meet its current day-to-day financial obligations.

4   D   Lengthening the maturity schedule of financing means putting in place longer term borrowing agreements with its financiers which would thereby provide a stand-by (D). Lowering the availability of cash or cash equivalents (A) would be unhelpful. Shortening the maturity schedule of financing would increase the risk of facilities not being renewed, further threatening the availability of standby funds (B). Investing in non-current assets (C) would reduce cash or absorb borrowing capacity so would not assist at all.

5   A   An aggressive policy implies financing long-term needs with short-term funds which would reduce liquidity but increase profitability (A) due to the cheaper short-term debt relative to long-term debt: decreased liquidity = increased risk.

6   B,D,I

The bank is expected to act with the utmost good faith in its relationship with the customer	Fiduciary
The bank asks the customer to secure a loan with a charge over the customer's assets	Mortgagor/ Mortgagee
The bank accepts the customer's property for storage in its safe deposit and undertakes to take reasonable care to safeguard it against loss or damage	Bailor/ Bailee

7   C   The capital markets consist of primary markets and secondary markets. New securities are issued on primary markets (C) whilst secondary markets (B) allow investors to buy existing securities or sell securities that they hold. Money markets (D) provide short term debt financing and investment. Futures markets (A) provide standardised futures contracts to buy or sell a particular commodity or financial instrument at a pre-determined price in the future.

8   C   Venture capitalists often will want a place on the board to secure their investment.

9   D   Financial intermediary is the general term for anyone who carries out this function. Business angels, merchant bankers and venture capitalists may all act as financial intermediaries.

10   D   Money market. The AIM and the London Stock Exchange are both examples of capital markets.

11   A   This is the UK central bank, and not an institutional investor.

12 C Venture capital is generally most appropriate for new investments with above average risk. Renovation of an existing facility is a part of the ongoing activity of the business, and is unlikely to have much impact on the overall level of returns. It is therefore unlikely to be appropriate for a venture capital investment.

13 D No new shares are issued in an introduction (A) and so there is no need to underwrite. An offer for sale by tender (B) would not normally need underwriting since the issue price reflects the value of the shares as perceived by the market. Underwriting would only be necessary if there is a risk that there will be under-subscription even at the minimum price. It is unnecessary to underwrite a placing (C) since a purchaser for the shares is arranged in the issue process. Although a rights issue (D) should not need underwriting in theory, since all the shares are being offered to existing shareholders, in practice it will usually be underwritten. This is to ensure that sufficient funds are raised from the issue, even if the rights are not fully exercised.

14 A A financial intermediary is a party that brings together providers and users of finance, either as broker or principal. Although the government may provide information on sources of finance and opportunities for investment, it will not normally broker a specific relationship. Pension funds (C) hold deposits on behalf of pension scheme members and invest them so as to provide funds to pay for their future pensions. They are therefore providing a link between the providers and users of finance. Building societies (B) and clearing banks (D) take deposits from savers, which are used to lend to other parties so as to produce a satisfactory rate of return. They are therefore linking together surplus units with deficit units in the economy.

15 C Rights issues are the only mechanism which cannot be used to obtain a stock exchange listing.

16 D Prudential control (D) refers to the regulation and monitoring of banks and other financial institutions by the Bank of England, the Treasury etc. Financial intermediaries provide advice and information to investors on available investment opportunities and their associated risks and returns (A). Intermediaries reduce investment risks (B) for individuals by creating an investment portfolio. Maturity transformation (C) overcomes the problem of matching the time periods for which a company or individual needs funds with the time periods over which investors wish to invest.

17 C Shares become more readily marketable when they are quoted. Not all plcs are quoted companies (D) and quoted companies face increased disclosure requirements (A), not reduced ones. The size of dividend does not depend on whether a company is quoted (B).

18 A Under a finance lease, the risks and rewards of ownership are transferred to the lessee, who will therefore normally be responsible for maintenance.

19 A Cash generated from retained earnings (A) is the source of finance that the majority of companies prefer traditionally. This is because it is simple, no recourse has to be made to the shareholders, and the control structure of the company is unaffected. New share issues (B) are expensive and risky. They are normally only undertaken when large amounts of new capital are required. Rights issues (C) are cheaper and easier to arrange than new share issues. However they must be priced attractively to ensure that enough shareholders will exercise their rights to make the issue a success. Bank borrowings (D) are a major source of finance since debt finance is generally cheaper and easier to arrange than equity, but it lacks the simplicity of using cash from retained earnings.

20 C An operating lease is a short-term contract which may not last for the full life of the asset. The lessor owns the asset. A, B and D are all common features of finance leases.

21 C Venture capital can be appropriate for a management buyout. Venture capital is high risk (A), and is not normally available to listed companies (B). It normally takes the form of equity finance, although it may take the form of debt finance (D).

22 D A property mortgage (D) is generally for a term longer than five years, and this is therefore a long-term source of finance.

23 A Interest is only paid on the amount borrowed, not on the full facility.

24 D This is a letter of credit. A bill of exchange (A) is drawn by one party on another (not necessarily by a bank). An export guarantee (B) is insurance against defaults on exports. A banker's draft (C) is a cheque drawn by a bank on one of its own bank accounts.

25 C Deciding what credit limits the client should give customers.

26 A Short-term cash surpluses will not normally be invested in equities owing to the risks associated with achieving a return over a short period.

27 B At this stage in their lives people generally aim to build up their retirement 'nest-eggs'. As their children are grown their expenditure is not so high, and they have generally already bought property and established careers.

28 C An individual with a high priority short- to medium-term financial objective and money to invest in respect of this will want to minimise risk and will accept a lower return as a result.

29 C Commercial paper. Commercial paper is a source of finance for banks and companies with good credit ratings.

30 C Financial instruments with maturities of less than one year are traded in the money market.

31 D Both ii and iv. The bond can be sold in a capital market and a secondary market.

32 A The long term interest rate is normally but not always higher than the short-term rate.

33 C The Bank of England's Financial Policy Committee seeks to take action to remove or reduce systemic risks in the UK financial system as a whole. Its Monetary Policy Committee aims to influence the quantity and price of money in the UK economy. The Bank of England's Prudential Regulation Authority is part of the 'twin peaks' regulatory regime for the financial services industry, the other part being the Financial Conduct Authority which is independent of the Bank of England.

Chapter 9: The professional accountant

1　B　The accountancy profession is concerned with providing measurement, disclosure or provision of assurance about financial information that helps managers, investors, tax authorities and other decision makers make resource allocation decisions.

　　　　(A) relates to financial reporting; (C) to management accounting; and (D) to financial management.

2　B　Expenses are matched with revenue earned under this basis of accounting because transactions and other events are recognised when they occur rather than when the related cash-flow is either paid or received. (A), (C) and (D) all relate in some way to cash flow.

3　B　According to fundamental accounting principles, when there is uncertainty caution must be exercised so as not to overstate assets nor understate liabilities – the prudence principle. When an amount is insignificant in the specific context it can be omitted – the materiality principle (A). Companies are allowed to change accounting policies if by so doing a fairer presentation is achieved (C). The inventory valuation method(s) used should be disclosed in the notes to the financial statements (D).

4　B,F

It is assumed that the company will continue on long enough to carry out its objectives and commitments, so non-current assets are shown at cost less depreciation	Going concern
A very large company's financial statements have the amounts rounded to the nearest £1,000	Materiality

5　B　The accounting principle that states that an item in the financial statements would make a difference if its omission or misstatement would mislead the reader of the financial statements under consideration is the materiality principle.

6　B　Accrued revenue is revenue that, as at the reporting date, has been earned but not yet received. If it was included it would boost the revenue figure, it would therefore boost the retained earnings figure and it would boost the current assets figure (as this is where accrued revenue is recorded).

7　B　The consistency principle states a company should use the same accounting methods and procedures from period to period.

8　A,C,F

　　　　Some areas of public practice are 'reserved' and so there are specific additional requirements for professional accountants engaged in them. The three areas are statutory audit, investment business and insolvency work.

9　A　Integrity – John has clearly breached the code by submitting a false application. He has acted neither with honesty nor integrity. He has, in fact, cheated and possibly gained an advantage over other candidates who could have been better qualified.

10   B,C,F

Receiving a benefit in the form of goods, services or hospitality from a client is permissible provided all receipts are declared, including their origin and value	False
You should not accept hospitality from clients because accepting such gifts threatens objectivity	True
Although you are prohibited from accepting most benefits such as gifts, it is perfectly in order to accept this type of hospitality from a client	False

Accepting such a large amount of hospitality clearly threatens the objectivity of the senior partner. It might have been in order to accept a gift or hospitality of nominal value in certain circumstances.

11   D   The main breach of the ICAEW Code of Ethics that she is proposing is in relation to confidentiality, including improper disclosure and improper use of information.

12   B   Encroachment, intimacy and self-promotion are incorrect.

13   A,D,E

An objective attitude towards a client is subject to self-interest or familiarity threats as a consequence of family or other close personal or business relationships	True
Where a close personal relationship exists between a member and someone in a client organisation, that person can continue to act for the company providing sufficient safeguards are in place	False
You should not personally take part in a company audit if you have worked for that company within two years of the period of the audit	True

Your friend and colleague is in breach of ethical principles in two ways. Her objectivity is threatened by her close personal relationship with the managing director. In addition, it is in breach of the guidelines for her to be involved in the audit of a business in which she has recently been employed or served as an officer.

14   A,D,E

There is a self-interest threat and an advocacy threat to Dark & Co.

Attending the social event may be inappropriate as Dark & Co as auditor may be seen as supporting Sports Galore Ltd in this venture – the advocacy threat. Gordon owning shares in the company may create a self-interest threat – he may be more interested in the value of the shares than providing a 'correct' opinion on the financial statements.

15   A   Revenue is recorded when goods or services are delivered whether or not cash has been received.

16   B   The ICAEW Code of Ethics is a framework- or ethics-based approach, which is the opposite of the compliance-, rule- or tick-box-based approach seen in other jurisdictions such as the US.

17   A   The fundamental principles form the bedrock of professional judgements and practice (A). It does not mean that the principles are easy (B). Taking the approach of mere compliance (C) and/or of following rules (D) is the exact opposite of what the fundamental principles represent.

18   A,C,F

Disciplinary proceedings   – Yes

Accounting principles   – Yes

The profession's interest   – No

Applying accounting principles is an aspect of technical competence. Disciplinary proceedings are relevant when there has been a failure of technical competence and/or professional responsibility. The profession's interest has no impact.   SAMPLE PAPER

19   B   The Companies Act 2006 states that a company secretary of a plc shall be a member of
           ICAEW (or certain other bodies) or a solicitor or barrister.   SAMPLE PAPER

20   A,D,F

Be a member of a recognised supervisory body	True
Be either a body corporate or a partnership	False
Hold a recognised qualification obtained in the UK	False

      Sole practitioners can be appointed as statutory auditors and certain overseas qualifications
      may be recognised. The other statement is correct.   SAMPLE PAPER

21   C   Enforcement of contracts is clearly a legal matter requiring the attention of the company's
           director of legal services.   SAMPLE PAPER

22   A, C and D

      The fundamental principles established by the ICAEW Code of Ethics are integrity, objectivity,
      professional competence and due care, confidentiality and professional behaviour.
                                                                                          SAMPLE PAPER

1   C   A consent order (C) is offered when there is a case to answer but the case is not so serious as to involve options (A) or (B). Publicity under a consent order would be exactly the same as under a Disciplinary Committee order (D).

2   A   The Department may refer the matter straight to the professional discipline team at FRC under the Accountancy Scheme in these circumstances.

3   D   Conciliation means trying to find a practical solution to a problem and will always precede other measures such as investigation and disciplinary proceedings.

4   B   If members disagree with a decision of the Disciplinary Committee (rather than the Investigation Committee) then cases might be referred to the Appeal Committee (A). Neither the Financial Reporting Council (C) nor the Prudential Regulation Authority (D) is relevant in this context.

5   D   The term 'accountant' has no special position in law (A). There is no legal requirement for an accountant to be a paid up member of the CCAB (B). She can call herself an accountant and she can offer all accountancy services except in the three reserved areas where specific levels of competence are demanded (C, D).

6   A   In areas other than audit, such as (B), (C) and (D), the FRC does not have statutory powers.

7   A   The FRC's Professional Oversight team in its Conduct Division also oversees regulation of the actuarial profession.

8   A,C

The CCAB has five members	True
The CCAB provides a forum in which matters affecting the profession as a whole can be discussed and co-ordinated and enables the profession to speak with a unified voice to government	True

9   B,C,F

Expertise – No (it should be professional competence and due care)

Confidentiality – Yes

Reliability – No (it should be integrity)

10   B,C,E

Anyone is free to advertise as an 'accountant' and offer the full range of accountancy services, with no exceptions	Not correct
ICAEW members are open to competition from anyone, whether professionally qualified or not, who chooses to enter the market	Correct
There is no legal requirement for an accountant to be a paid-up member of one of the CCAB bodies	Correct

The first statement is incorrect because although anyone is free to advertise as an accountant, there are three 'reserved' areas of business (insolvency, investment and statutory audit) where statute demands specific levels of competence.

11 A,D,E

Dealing with professional misconduct by its members	True
Acting as adviser to the government on necessary legislative changes	False
Confirming eligibility for the performance of reserved activities under statutory powers delegated by the government	True

The Financial Reporting Council is the body that acts as an adviser to the government on necessary legislative changes.

12 A   The FRC consists of Conduct Division and the Codes and Standards Division.

13 A,C,F

Protect the public from being misled or from suffering from abuse of power through knowledge or monopoly	True
Ensure that technical, educational and ethical standards are maintained at a level the public has a right to expect	True
Protect vested interests from competition so as to maintain public confidence that the public interest is being safeguarded	False

Regulation of professions should specifically not protect vested interests from competition.

14 A,D Tribunal hearings are normally open to the public except in exceptional circumstances where the Tribunal decides that this would not be in the interests of justice.

15 B,C Rules of evidence are less strict than in a court.

16 A,C,F,G

Fine the firm	True
Exclude the firm from membership of the ICAEW	True
Offer an unpublicised caution	False
Take away a member's practising certificate	True

The offering of an unpublicised caution is a course of action open to the Investigation Committee at an earlier stage in the disciplinary process.

17 A,C,F

Has departed from guidance	True
Has brought the ICAEW into disrepute	True
Is in breach of a principle	False

The third option should refer to the breach of a regulation rather than a principle.

18 D   The FRC, via the Conduct Division's Financial Reporting Review Panel, investigates departures from relevant accounting standards by large companies such as those listed on the LSE.

19 A   The Financial Reporting Council's professional discipline team in its Conduct Division investigates specifically those cases that raise important issues affecting the public interest.

SAMPLE PAPER

Chapter 11: Governance, corporate responsibility, sustainability and ethics

1   A, B and C

   Empathy and accountability were not among them. The other two were courage and openness.

2   B   (A), (C) and (D) are all characteristics of bank-based financial systems.

3   A   Household preference for equity (more risk) rather than bank deposits (less risk) means that equity finance is likely to dominate the financing of businesses.

4   D   Under a unitary board structure there would not be a supervisory board (B). The reporting responsibility is to shareholders (D), not to other directors (A) nor employees (C).

5   B   Financial intermediation overcomes the problem of asymmetric information associated with direct financing.

6   B   The separation of ownership and control creates a situation where managers act as the agents of owners (shareholders), who are, therefore, the principals.

7   B, C

| The practices and procedures for trying to ensure that a company is run in such a way that it achieves its objectives | Does not match |
| A set of relationships between a company's management, its board, its shareholders and other stakeholders | Does match |

8   B   This definition of the aim of corporate governance is the broadest possible perspective – the public policy perspective.

9   B,C,F

   The first statement is false (B) – Germany has a two-tier system comprising a management board and a supervisory board (C). The supervisory board rather than the management board has the powers to approve or not approve the financial statements and dividends declared (F).

10   B   (A) should read transparent and efficient markets, not reporting. (C) should read all shareholders, not just major shareholders. (D) should read timely rather than real time.

11   A,D   The first statement is true as set out by the International Society of Business, Economics and Ethics. The second statement is false – social responsibility is measured by how far the organisation protects the interests of those who have non-contractual relationships, such as the public at large.

12   A   Corporate ethics are principally moulded by society's expectations.

13   C   As a whistleblower she would be protected by the Public Interest Disclosure Act.

14   B, C and D

   (B), (C) and (D) all relate to a generic financial system. Governance structures and regulators may or may not exist within a particular system, but they are by no means basic elements of it.

15   B, C and E

   The lack of codes of practice and regulation contribute to rather than detract from the efficiency of markets in resource allocation.

16   A   The OECD (B) produced Principles of Corporate Governance, but it does not have UK responsibility for the promotion of high standards of corporate governance. The CCAB (C) and the Bank of England (D) have no such responsibility.

17 B   Rather than simply looking to do the minimum required, the company will look to exceed it, in relation to all stakeholders not merely shareholders.

18 A and D

The separation of ownership and control refers to the classic 'agency problem', in which investors (shareholders) who own the company delegate to managers (as agents) responsibility for running the business for the ultimate benefit of the owners. Corporate governance is fundamentally concerned with ensuring that the managers act as the owners would want them to.   SAMPLE PAPER

19 A   The stewardship approach requires that directors should act at all times in the company's best interests, not in their own. This is a resolution of the agency problem. Allowing shareholders to see detailed accounting records on request, holding monthly meetings to answer shareholders' queries and consulting shareholders over difficult management decisions are not factors that are required by the stewardship approach, though a company can choose to enforce such procedures if it wants.   SAMPLE PAPER

Chapter 12: Corporate governance

1   A,D,E,G

Satisfying himself on the integrity of the company's financial information	Responsible
Reporting on the performance of the company	Not responsible
Determining appropriate levels of remuneration for executive directors	Responsible
Satisfying himself that financial controls and systems of risk management are robust and defensible	Responsible

The role of a non-executive director is to monitor the reporting of performance by the executive directors. These rules are set out in the supporting principle for the main principle A4 (leadership: non-executive directors) in the Code.

2   D   This is set out in the provision supporting B1 (effectiveness: the composition of the board) in the Code.

3   B,D

Being outside the FTSE 100, the UK Corporate Governance Code does not apply to Jumpers plc	False
Being in the FTSE 350, Jumpers plc must not depart from any of the UK Corporate Governance Code's requirements	False

The Code applies to all FTSE 350 companies, but whilst they are expected to comply with the main principles, non-compliance with supporting principles and provisions is allowed provided it is properly explained.

4   B   This is stated explicitly in provisions supporting main principle D1 (remuneration: level and components) in the Code.

5   B   A company should seek to improve corporate governance by ensuring that the chairman and chief executive are different individuals in order to prevent one person from having unfettered powers of decision in line with main principle A2 (leadership: division of responsibilities) of the Code.

6   A   This is set out in principles supporting main principle B6 (effectiveness: evaluation) of the Code.

7   A,C,F

Link remuneration to corporate and individual performance: main principle D1 (remuneration: level and components of remuneration)

Establish a formal and transparent procedure for developing policy on executive remuneration and for fixing the remuneration packages of individual directors: main principle D2 (remuneration: procedure)

The auditors are not required to comment on the equity of the remuneration but should ensure that there is appropriate disclosure in the financial statements.

8   C   This is set out in provisions supporting main principle D2 (remuneration: procedure) of the Code.

9   B,C,F

'Non-executive directors of FTSE 350 companies, once appointed, only need to be submitted for re-election every three years'. This is not true – in the FTSE 350 they must be submitted for annual election just like executive directors (principle supporting main principle B7 effectiveness; re-election)	False
'The board's responsibility to present a fair, balanced and understandable assessment of company performance extends not only to annual financial statements but also to interim reports'. This is in the principles supporting main principle C1 (accountability: financial and business reporting)	True
UK Corporate Governance Code states that directors' service contracts should not exceed three years – This is not true as the Code recommends that contract or notice periods should not exceed one year; if a longer period is agreed for a new director then this should be reduced to one year or less as soon as possible (provisions supporting main principle D1: level and components of remuneration)	False

10   C   This is set out in provisions supporting main principle E2 (relations with shareholders: constructive use of the AGM) of the Code.

11   D   This is set out in provisions supporting C3 (accountability: audit committee and auditors) of the Code.

12   C   The company can be flexible in how it applies the UK Corporate Governance Code (C). Non-FTSE 350 companies may depart even from the main principles in particular circumstances provided their non-compliance is explained (A). The company will be expected to adhere to the requirements of the Code by virtue of being listed (B) and (D).

13   A   The directors have to state that the financial statements are prepared on the going concern basis, if this is the case.

14   B   This is set out in provisions supporting main principle B1 (effectiveness: the composition of the board) of the Code.

15   B   Both the directors and the management have responsibility as senior management to protect the company against fraud and irregularity.

16   B   Provisions supporting main principle C3 (accountability: audit committee and auditors) of the Code clearly state that the requirement is for independent non-executive directors, with at least one member of the committee needing to have recent and relevant financial experience, but not all of them.

17   C   The entire board is responsible: main principle C2 (accountability: risk management and internal control) of the Code.

18   B   As a full-time executive director of a FTSE 100 company, the guidance as updated in 2010 is that she should not be permitted to take on the chairmanship of another FTSE 100 company. This revision is set out in provisions supporting main principle B3 (effectiveness: commitment) of the Code.

19   D   This is set out in provisions supporting main principle C3 (accountability: audit committee and auditors) of the Code.

20   B   This is set out in provisions supporting main principle D1 (remuneration: level and components of remuneration) of the Code.

21   D   One of the provisions supporting main principle B1 (effectiveness: the composition of the board) is that at least 50% of the board, excluding the chairman, should be independent non-executive directors.   SAMPLE PAPER

22   C   One of the specific roles and responsibilities accorded to the audit committee by the Code is the development and implementation of policy on the engagement of the external auditor to supply non-audit services. This is contained in provisions supporting main principle C3 (accountability: audit committee and auditors).   SAMPLE PAPER

23   A   It is the shareholders who actually vote to appoint the external auditors (A), although this is usually on the recommendation of the audit committee (B) and the board (C). The finance director (D) may be heavily involved in the conduct of the audit but should not be actively involved in appointment except as a member of the board.   SAMPLE PAPER

24   A   An effective internal audit function has, as a fundamental requirement, to maintain its independence at all times.   SAMPLE PAPER

1   A   With normal goods, a rise in incomes will be accompanied by a rise in demand for them as opposed to a fall in demand for inferior goods. The existence of complements and substitutes have no effect in this context.

2   C   The effect of a price rise in one good is to make the prices of other goods relatively cheaper. The resultant shift in demand towards the relatively cheaper goods is an example of the substitution effect.

3   A   If potatoes are a Giffen good, then an increase in the price of potatoes will cause an increase in demand for potatoes.

4   C   Complements are goods that tend to be bought and used together, so that an increase in demand for one is likely to cause an increase in demand for the other. (A), (B) and (C) are substitutes rather than complements.

5   D   If X is a complement of Y then they tend to be consumed together, so if demand for Y falls as a result of the increase in its price then demand for X will also fall.

6   B,D Both statements are false. Demand for an inferior good will fall with rises in income as consumers shift to better quality goods that they can now afford with their higher incomes. Demand for the inferior product could exist because of its price and the level of incomes, not just because of advertising.

7   C   A normal good which has become increasingly unfashionable will see its demand curve shift to the left, a fall in market price and a fall in quantity supplied.

8   B   With a natural monopoly, fixed costs will be high, marginal costs will be low (B) and economies of *scale* (rather than *scope*) provide an effective barrier to entry.

9   C   Negative externalities (C) are an example of market failure because they represent situations where the private costs of an activity differ from the social costs of the activity. Economic booms (A) and Giffen goods (D) are not market failures. No market failure is apparent in (B).

10 D   Zero cross-elasticity means the goods are unrelated.

11 A   +0.065/–0.04 = –1.625

12 B   A price below the market equilibrium price will attract demand but deter suppliers.

13 A   A vertical straight line implies that the supply of the Ledo is fixed whatever price is offered.

14 A   When factor costs rise demand contracts (moves along the demand curve) since the price goes up, and the supply curve shifts to the left (contracts).

15 A   The key differentiator here is the large number of competing sellers. The earlier issues identified in the question are shared by both monopolistic competition and oligopoly, but it is the large number of sellers in the market that defines this market specifically as monopolistic competition.

16 B, C and E

    Suppliers are price-takers meaning that they can sell as much as they supply but only if they sell at the market-determined equilibrium price (E). Differentiated products (D) are a market imperfection creating imperfect rather than perfect competition.

17 B   External economies of scale arise by virtue of the market for the product growing, enabling greater levels of business across which to spread the company's costs.

18 B   Proportional change in quantity demanded = 40/150 × 100 = –26.6%

    Proportional change in price = 1/9 × 100 = 11.1%

    PED = –26.6/11.1 = –2.40   SAMPLE PAPER

19   A, E

      Demand for the good – Fall

      Supply of the good – Rise

      Suppliers will be encouraged to supply at that price so supply will increase, whilst at a price above the market equilibrium price demand will fall.   SAMPLE PAPER

20   A   With normal goods, if incomes rise demand for the product will rise and this will be the case regardless of the existence of either substitutes or complements.   SAMPLE PAPER

21   D   The basic economic problem is one of allocating scarce resources and economics is the study of how those scarce resources are or should be used.

22   C   Management is a specialised type of labour. A, B and D are factors of production; the missing factor is land.

23   D   The correct answer should be: Land is rewarded with rent.

24   D   Technical improvements could apply at any scale of operations.

25   D   The relationship between changes in income and changes in consumption.

26   A   When an economy booms, it reaches a turning point and goes into recession. The recession deepens into a depression. Eventually, there is another turning point in the economy, and the business cycle goes into recovery and then back into boom, and so on.

27   A   Recession and declining demand go together. Inflation and declining demand do not. The trade balance is likely to improve due to a decrease in demand for imports.

28   A   B, C and D will all be measures which reduce the demand for goods and services. Public expenditure (D) represents the government's own demand. Bank lending (C) is largely used for spending on goods and services by the people who borrow the money. Higher value added tax (B) could increase total spending on goods and services **inclusive** of the tax, but spending **net** of tax will fall, and this should result in a reduction in demand-pull inflation. Lower interest rates (A) is likely to result in higher consumer borrowing and even stronger demand-pull inflation.

29   D   This is an example of demand pull inflation.

30   B   Low interest rates will encourage spending rather than saving. Investment will be encouraged because the opportunity cost of investing is reduced.

31   D   Fiscal policy is concerned with the government's tax income, expenditure and borrowing (to make up the difference between income and expenditure).

32   C   It is aggregate supply in the economy which is at issue.

33   D   Higher taxation will tend to reduce consumer spending. Higher import tariffs might result in greater consumer expenditure on imports inclusive of tariffs, but the volume and the net-of-tariff value of imports purchased will fall. Higher social security payments will give consumers more cash to spend.

1   D   An externality is an adverse social consequence which the private producer has no incentive to minimise.

2   A   Innovation in this context is where regulation serves to trigger the discovery and introduction of new procedures and technologies – the 'innovation effect', as a basis for competitive advantage in an industry.

3   A   Collusion can lead to a fine of up to 10% of annual global revenues.

4   A   The tax on cigarettes may not raise as much revenue as anticipated in the years to come because the demand for cigarettes is likely to become more elastic over time. Price elasticity nearly always increases over time and will reduce the tax revenue. People can change their behaviour given enough time.

5   A   Chapter 1 of the Competition Act 1998 specifically deals with anti-competitive agreements.

6   B   Government intervention in a market economy can lead to an increase in economic welfare if the market mechanism has failed to allow for externalities. The government setting a minimum or maximum price above the equilibrium price would be ineffective. Demand for inferior goods falls as incomes rise.

7   A,B   The Competition Commission cannot initiate any inquiries itself (C), nor can individual companies (D) nor the London Stock Exchange (E).

8   D   Restricting supply (via quota) will cause the price to rise.

9   A   Monopoly is the antithesis of perfect competition and is, therefore, a market imperfection.

10   B,C,D

     Imposing unfair purchase or selling prices would be considered as an abuse where the business is in a dominant position but transfer pricing (A) refers to the pricing of goods and services within a multi-divisional organisation, particularly in regard to cross-border transactions.

11   D   A cartel is most likely where there are few producers in the market, each of them producing a similar product.

12   B   The main effect of anti-monopoly enforcement is deterrence – there is little innovation effect.

13   B   Tending towards a perfect market through increased competition should lead to allocative efficiency and lower prices.

14   B,C,F

     The first and third statements are false, but the second statement is true – anti-monopoly legislation favours competition, but where competition is not possible, then market regulation is used to compensate for the lack of competition.

15   C   Redistribution of wealth is an attempt to address lack of equity.

16   C   Collusion is an example of market power exerted by a few suppliers.   SAMPLE PAPER

17   B,C,F

     Limiting production markets – No (this is an abuse of a dominant position, covered by Chapter II of the Act)

     Agreeing with another organisation to limit competition – Yes

     Restricting technical developments – No (this again is an abuse of a dominant position)
                    SAMPLE PAPER

ICAEW

REVIEW FORM – BUSINESS AND FINANCE: Question Bank

Your ratings, comments and suggestions would be appreciated on the following areas of
this Question Bank

	Very useful	Useful	Not useful
Number of questions in each section	☐	☐	☐
Standard of answers	☐	☐	☐
Amount of guidance on exam technique	☐	☐	☐
Quality of marking guides	☐	☐	☐

	Excellent	Good	Adequate	Poor
Overall opinion of this Question Bank	☐	☐	☐	☐

Please return completed form to:

The Learning Team
Learning and Professional Department
ICAEW
Metropolitan House
321 Avebury Boulevard
Milton Keynes
MK9 2FZ
E learning@icaew.com

For space to add further comments please see overleaf.

REVIEW FORM (continued)

TELL US WHAT YOU THINK

Please note any further comments and suggestions/errors below.